Amber & Gabe

1 yr in the book of your life as husband and wife has been completed! Keep building on your solid foundation. Keep God first!

Love

Mom & Dad

Marriage from A to Z

Principles For A Successful Marriage

Carolyn Tatem

FOREVER
publishing

FOREVER PUBLISHING

Marriage from A to Z (Principles for a Successful Marriage)

Copyright ©2010, 2015 by Carolyn Tatem

Requests for information should be sent to: Marriagefromatoz@gmail.com

First published by Author House   8/24/2010
Second published by Forever Publishing 7/09/2015

Library of Congress Control Number: 2015910925

ISBN: 978-0-9962851-0-0 (softcover)

Printed in the United States of America

FOREWARD

We have given our lives to helping married couples experience their dream marriage. We have been blessed to be around great communicators and numerous books about marriage. However, not all books are created equal. Carolyn has done a brilliant job with *Marriage From A to Z*. We find most people are not interested in simply hearing statistics about marriage; they want someone who is willing to be transparent about the real struggles of building marital intimacy. Carolyn does not disappoint. Her vulnerability about the challenges in her own marriage blended with biblical truth will engage you and enable you to identify.

We have known Carolyn and her husband William for several years now and they are passionately devoted to helping married couples develop strong relationships. They model an authentic marriage and this is frequently exhibited in their matching colors whenever they go on a date together. *Marriage From A to Z* is an easy read, packed with chunks of practical tips that will enable you to achieve your dream marriage.

Dr. Johnny and Lezlyn Parker

Former Speakers of FamilyLife Marriage Conferences
Chaplains of the Washington Redskins and Washington Mystics

DEDICATION

First, I would like to dedicate this book to my husband, William Tatem. William and I have been married for eleven wonderful years. Our marriage and our relationship with God have given me the principles for this book. Second, I dedicate this book to my beautiful gifts from God, Torre, Ciara, and Ahmad Tatem. I thank God for the privilege of being your mom. You are a joy! Thank you for your support and encouragement as I worked on this book. I love you and hope that one day God will bless you with mates with whom you are able to practice the principles in this book.

ACKNOWLEDGMENTS

I thank God for allowing me to be His daughter and giving me everything that I needed to write this book.

I am so grateful for all of my family members. I especially want to thank my Mom (Shirley), for bringing me into this world when she could have aborted me. Grandpa and Grandma (Edward & Delores), thank you for helping to raise me and always being willing to care for my children.

I want to thank my church family (First Baptist Church of Glenarden), and all of my friends who have prayed and been supportive of this project. It was a newlywed couple (Christopher & Keisha Wiggans) who first gave me the challenge to write down all of the marriage principles and put them in a book. I want to thank the Queen Esther Ministry for their prayers and encouragement throughout this journey.

In addition, I want to thank the following who have impacted my life so much that I was able to write the principles for this book.

Evelyn Johnson-Taylor – Thanks for mentoring me and serving as my accountability partner while writing this book.

Pastor John K. Jenkins, Sr. and First Lady Trina Jenkins – Thanks for the godly example that you set, the opportunities that you have given me to serve and helping to develop me into a dynamic disciple.

Reverend Clarence and Reverend Mary Eldridge – Thank you for counseling and depositing God's principles into William and me. Also, for supporting and believing in us.

Reverend Johnny and Mrs. Lezlyn Parker – Thank you for being willing to write the foreward for this book.

Michelle Singletary – Thanks for taking the time out of your busy schedule to give me feedback and encouragement for this book.

The late Bishop Lewis T. Tait, Sr. and Mrs. Christine Tait – Thank you for introducing me to Christ and teaching me how to be a Christian young lady.

Dennis and Barbara Rainey – Thank you for Family Life Ministry. It has helped to teach William and I about marriage God's way.

CONTENTS

INTRODUCTION

As a teenager, I can remember daydreaming about my wedding day. I watched weddings on television and participated in so many weddings, wondering when my day would come and who the groom would be. Through the years, I would try to guess who I would end up marrying, and each time I was wrong. I didn't end up meeting Mr. Right until I was about twenty-seven years old.

We met while volunteering to work with teens in the Youth Ministry at First Baptist Church of Glenarden. He fits the image that I had in mind: he is tall, dark, and handsome! We both volunteered our time and served in the Youth Ministry for about two years. After two years, William told me how he felt about me. He said that he had been admiring me for two years and that it was finally time to tell me how he felt. We courted, went to premarital counseling for six months, and were married in August 1998. In the beginning of our marriage, we asked God to use us to work with other couples. We started a fellowship for engaged and newlywed couples in our home and have been serving in Couple's Ministry for over eleven years.

I am not writing this book because I have a perfect marriage. I am writing because over the eleven years that my husband and I have been married and serving other couples, we have learned so much. Yet, we are still learning. There are so many principles that we have embraced in our marriage that are working well; therefore, we share them with couples who come into our midst. However, we want to share the principles with all married couples. Perhaps something will be shared to bless your marriage or someone you know. Marriage is a wonderful institution, and it should reflect the beautiful relationship that Christ has with the church. I hope that the principles shared in this book will bless your marriage or help you prepare for marriage. Enjoy!

CHAPTER ONE
THE *A* PRINCIPLES

ACCEPTANCE

What you see is what you get! Oftentimes, we see exactly what and who we are getting. However, we get married and then immediately try to change our mate. When the change does not occur the way we would like, we instantly have a problem. We must accept each other for who we are, the way that we are. My husband was raised in the country, and I was raised in the city. There are some things that I just have to accept because of the way that he was raised, and there are some things about me that he just has to accept. It is okay to suggest changes, but the problem arises when your mate does not want to change and you develop an attitude. Certain things are clear before you marry but you still marry with the hopes that things will change.

I had to accept the fact that William was accustomed to life in the country. One of the things that was so different from the way that I was raised is that he is used to driving up in front of his family's house, getting out of the car without locking the doors, and leaving his keys inside of the car. In addition to the keys, he would tell me its okay to leave my purse in the car. The way that I was brought up, you did not leave anything visible in the car. You take your keys with you, roll up the windows, lock all of the doors, and you definitely would not leave your purse within view. The smallest differences in the way that a person is raised have a lot to do with who that person is and how he or she thinks. It is so important for us to get to know our mates; then we can better understand why they are the way that they are and why they do some of the things that they do.

You must be willing to accept your mate just the way that he or she is. Prayer is the key to seeing changes in your mate. As much as we would like to be able to snap our fingers and have some things changed, we don't have the power to change others. The only person we can change is ourselves. We must rely on God to make the changes in our mates. Therefore, accept your wife or husband just the way that she or he is.

ADMIT

Some of the most difficult words for people to say are, "I was wrong, will you forgive me?" Admitting that you are wrong is a big step! We all have experienced being wrong. No one is perfect; however, we must be willing to admit when we are wrong. We can't be right all of the time. It takes humility to admit when you are wrong.

Be willing to say, "I was wrong," when situations arise and you know that you were wrong. Instead of admitting this, some people go on as if nothing has ever happened. This can be frustrating and may cause a problem later on. When you admit that you are wrong, ask for forgiveness, and then move on when the road is clear.

ANGER

"Be angry and do not sin!" (Ephesians 4:26) There is no doubt about it, something is going to be said or done in your marriage that will make you angry. The key is getting angry and not sinning. I can remember one of the first major arguments that William and I had after we got married. The argument was about how we were going to spend our Sunday afternoon after church. I thought that Sunday should always be a family day and spent together. My husband didn't completely agree.

One Sunday, after we went to church, we came home, and he wanted to go with the guys to a sporting event. I did not agree; I wanted us to be together, so I thought he should not go. However, it didn't matter to him, so he went anyway. I was so upset that I cried and spent the afternoon trying to figure out what I could do to let him know how upset I really was. My hope was that this wouldn't happen again. So when he came home, I really didn't want to be there, but I had no place to go. I didn't want everyone to know my business, and I was taught that when you have a disagreement, you do not go running back home to your family. Therefore, I hid in the basement. It took him a minute to find me, because normally, I would not be in the basement. After a few minutes of searching upstairs, he found me. We began to talk, and the next thing I knew, we kissed and made up.

I shared all of this to say that there are going to be times when you don't get your way; you won't like the way that something is said or done, so you get angry. However, it is what you do after the anger that causes a problem. I wanted to make him hurt like I was hurting. I didn't want to talk for a while, and I wanted to separate myself, just because I didn't get my way. Later, the Lord spoke to me and said, "Carolyn, there are going to be many days when you get angry, but you can't just shut down, stop talking, and go hide somewhere. You must learn to discuss the issue and move on in love."

I began to read the love chapter, 1 Corinthians 13, every day for thirty days so that I could get a better understanding of what love is and what my actions should be toward the man I love. Practicing God's love in the midst of being angry is a challenge, but His grace is sufficient for you.

APPRECIATION

It is a good thing to give thanks! Every mate needs to hear the words "thank you, I appreciate you, I appreciate this, or I appreciate that!" So often we take each other for granted, as if you are doing what you are supposed to be doing, so I don't need to say, "Thank you, honey," or express my appreciation. These words are so simple, but often go unspoken.

God uses gratitude to change our attitude. Gratitude that is verbally expressed is like fuel to an engine. When my husband expresses his appreciation, it makes me want to serve him more. Just simply saying thank you for having dinner ready this evening makes me want to have dinner ready the next evening. Ungratefulness can zap one's energy to serve.

There may be times when you have to serve even if you don't hear "Thank you" or "I appreciate you." When these times arise, just know that God is a God who sees and knows everything that we do. We must do everything as if we are working directly for the Lord. The Lord will show His appreciation by rewarding you. The Bible says that we must do the will of God from the heart, knowing that whatever good anyone does, he will receive the same from the Lord (Ephesians 6:6–8).

I have heard husbands say, "She doesn't do anything for me to appreciate" or vice versa. However, search harder and God will show you something for which you can express your appreciation. It could be as simple as "Thank you for coming home today; your presence means so much." Start with the little things, and before you know it, there will be bigger things.

ATTENTION

If someone were to ask you specific details about your mate based on yesterday, could you answer? What did your mate have on yesterday? Did you notice anything about his or her eyes? Was there anything different about their hair, hands, and so on? These questions may be hard to answer. Due to the busyness of the days, we often come and go from each other's presence without really paying attention to each other. Have you ever experienced being in the same house all day, but you are in different areas of the house? You are doing your thing and your husband is doing his thing. Days can go by and you haven't really given any attention to each other. The problem arises when these days turn into weeks and then the weeks into months. Before you know it, years have gone by and so much time has elapsed. Where did your attention go? If we are not careful, our attention goes into doing something else or someone else.

It is so important to give attention to your mate daily. Acknowledge each other when you leave and enter the home. Take time to greet each other. Find out what kind of day your mate is having; ask, "How are you feeling?" and "What are your priorities for the day?" Notice a new outfit, hairstyle, or any other changes that have been made. Give attention to your marriage by noticing your mate, spending quality time together, and communicating throughout the day. Always remember, if we don't want to give attention, somebody else will. Make time to study each other daily so that you can be in tune with your mate. Paying attention to your mate and your marriage can save you from having to pay later.

ATTITUDE

When I was coming up, I often heard the popular saying, "Your attitude determines your altitude." I have found this statement to be true and relevant to marriage. Your attitude about your marriage often determines how high your marriage will go and how long it will last. Many times people get married with the wrong attitude. They say, "If it doesn't work, I'll just get a divorce." Guess what? If this is your attitude, it probably will not work out. Anyone who starts a marriage with this type of attitude is bound for divorce. What you think triggers what you speak and how you act. Just saying, "If it doesn't work out, I'll get a divorce" puts you on dangerous ground. The Bible says that "death and life are in the power of the tongue" (Proverbs 18:21). So speak life in your marriage; don't let your attitude kill your marriage.

A marriage is a covenant relationship that was not meant to be broken. The covenant can only be broken through death. So when you tell your brain that if things don't go a certain way, you will divorce, as soon as a problem comes that takes you to the limit, divorce comes to mind. A marriage relationship that will last for any length of time will consist of ups and downs, highs and lows, sickness and health, seasons of plenty and seasons of lack. However, you must have an attitude of being married till death do you part. Take all exit signs out of your marriage. You may need to stop, yield, and then go, but don't exit. You can make it! Take a moment and examine your attitude about your marriage. Is it good? Are you in it for life? If not, I challenge you to get the right attitude. Say, "With God's help, we will be married till death do us part!" For with God, ALL THINGS ARE POSSIBLE! (Matthew 19:26)

CHAPTER TWO
THE *B* PRINCIPLES

BALANCE

I can remember a part of the wedding vows that state, "forsaking all others as long as we both shall live." We live in a world where there is so much to do. Oftentimes, we get married, we work, we have children, we are involved in various activities and our children are involved in various activities. We have to make time to spend with our family and our friends. Therefore, we spend our lives trying to allocate time in each area.

I believe the key to balance is having a daily relationship with Jesus Christ. One of my favorite Bible verses is Matthew 6:33. I live by this verse because it says, "Seek ye first the kingdom of God and His righteousness and all of these things will be added unto you." This verse speaks to me because it says that when I put God first, everything else will fall into place. As I spend daily time with the Lord, He speaks to me about all of the areas of my life. There have been times that I have had my morning time with God, and He will begin to speak to me about my husband, my children, family members, or friends. I have even had the Lord remind me, in my quiet time, that I haven't initiated intimacy with my husband. When I obey what the Lord reveals to me, I am always blessed. My husband will say, "What made you do that, or what made you initiate?" I have to give credit to God. You see, God wants us to have a successful marriage and family; therefore, when we spend time with Him, He reminds us of the things that we need to do to keep these relationships healthy.

It has been in my time with God that He has put ideas in my head that involve getting family members together. I have planned several dinners and celebrations because God placed the idea in my heart. Some of them were so creative I know that it was God's idea and not my own doing.

God will teach us how to balance, because relationships are important to Him. His Word teaches us that children are gifts from Him. We need balance so that we can properly attend to the gifts that He has given to us. If we don't balance ourselves and our time correctly, we lose precious time with the precious gifts that God has given to us. Our gifts are only young for a season; we must balance our lives accordingly.

One of the things that helped me in my earlier years of parenting was leaving my job to become a stay-at-home mom. I was home with Ciara and Ahmad for six years. During these years, my total focus was providing an atmosphere in the home where my husband would be happy to come, and my children would be nurtured and developed as godly seeds. Balance starts in the home. Children learn where our priorities are by how we treat them. The question that I constantly ask myself is, "Does my lifestyle, schedule, and the way that I spend my time say that my husband and children are first?" I constantly remind myself that Ciara and Ahmad are precious gifts from God and that He is holding me responsible for raising them. I want my actions toward them to say, "I value you because God values you." I never want my actions or schedule to say that I don't have time for them. Now that I work outside of the home, I have to work even harder to connect at home and make time to spend with Ciara and Ahmad. I want them to always know that no matter what we have to do, we will make time for the gifts that God has given to us. Balance is essential to developing, building, and maintaining relationships.

BEARING

In 1 Corinthians 13:7 it says that love bears all things. God is calling us to bear up and to bear with our mates. To bear up means to endure and face hardship bravely. To bear with means to be patient and forbearing. In today's world, we hear very little about couples who choose to bear up and more about couples who choose to give up. As soon as hardship comes in our marriage, our flesh wants to run away and give up, but God is calling more couples to bear ALL things.

Normally, bearing does not feel good to the flesh, but it is good for the spirit. In order to successfully bear all things, we truly need the help and power of God. Some situations and hardships are so difficult that one cannot continue in their normal strength. However, God will come in and strengthen you on every side. When you are weak, He becomes strong in you. Love bears all things!

BELIEVE

In January of 2002, I left my job to stay home and raise my two babies. Ciara was two years old and Ahmad was a newborn. It was a major adjustment because we had to transition from living off of two incomes to one income. I had no idea how this was going to work, but I believed that since God led me to come home to raise my own children, He would take care of us. I remember thinking that I couldn't trust my husband's job because his business went up and down. God told me not to trust in my husband's job but to trust in Him. So, I left my job and believed God like never before.

One day, Ciara came home with a homework assignment that required her to dream, and find a picture that represented her dream. She found a picture of Mickey Mouse and said her dream was to be able to take a trip to Disney World. When she shared her dream with me, I immediately thought, *Baby, I don't know if this dream will ever come true.* I knew that since we were living off of one income, this dream seemed so far-fetched. However, I never uttered anything negative to Ciara. I didn't want to kill her dream. I thought if she could believe, we could take the dream to God in prayer and see what happened. I told Ciara that God could make her dream come true.

About one year later, my husband started working for a company that provided transportation from place to place as a benefit to their employees and their immediate family members. As a result, we could travel to Florida free of charge. The only thing that we had to pay for was the hotel stay and the tickets to get into Disney World. To make a long story short, God made a way for us stay at a hotel and get tickets to go to Disney World. It was unbelievable! We had a wonderful vacation on one income because God provided. We weren't able to do this on two incomes, but God provided and made it happen on one income.

The lesson that I learned is to know that *all* things are possible if you believe. As couples, we should dream and believe in God to make our dreams a reality. Sometimes, we limit ourselves and our relationships because we are afraid to dream. God can handle our dreams. Pray about them, write them down, and believe in God. There is nothing that is too hard for Him. For faith is the substance of things hoped for, the evidence of things not seen (Hebrews 11:1). We don't have to see it or know how it is going to happen; we just need to believe. BELIEVE! All things are possible to those who believe.

BIBLE

Can you imagine going on a road trip without directions or a map? Let's say you live in Washington, D.C., and your destination is California. You have never been outside Washington but you decide to go to California. You get on the highway and just start driving. You hope that you will eventually get to California. How crazy does this sound?

Going to California without a map is just like getting married without directions. Marriage is an institution created by God, and the map is the Bible. He has given us principles to live by and to guide us on how to live as husband and wife. There are so many principles in God's word that teach us how to live. However, if we never read the Bible or listen to the word being preached, we will not know the direction that He wants for our marriage.

The scripture says, "My people are destroyed for lack of knowledge" (Hosea 4:6). Marriages are perishing today because of a lack of knowledge. When one does not know the principles of God, he or she cannot apply them to his or her marriage relationship. Application of the word of God is the real key. Sometimes, we go to church and hear the word, but when it comes to really applying the word, we just don't do it.

The Bible principle is all about a couple taking time to read God's word and apply the principles to their marriage. Each day, we should spend some time reading God's word. As we take in His word and ask Him how it should be applied, we will see a difference in our individual lives as well as our marriage. The way that God thinks is so much different from the way that we think. Therefore, we need to learn His ways and replace our way with His way of doing things. When we read and follow God's direction, we can get to the destination that He would have us reach. Otherwise, we can end up someplace totally different. Some read the newspaper every day to find out what is going on in the world but never pick up the Bible to find out what God wants to tell them. God gave us His word to teach us how to live and to teach us more about Him. Why not read it and apply it? If we want to have a successful marriage relationship, we must do it God's way. After all, He created marriage.

The Bible is God's holy word. It is truth and there are no mistakes in God's word. It was written by men who were inspired by God many years ago. When William and I united, we realized that we were entering God's holy institution called marriage. We also knew that we must live by the instructions and wishes of God, if we wanted the marriage to work. We understood that God created marriage and that following His instructions creates a successful marriage. Successful doesn't mean a perfect marriage, because we know that when two imperfect people come together, it doesn't equal a perfect marriage. However, when an imperfect husband and an imperfect wife are united and decide to follow God's perfect law, they can experience a successful marriage.

In Psalms Chapter 1, the Bible says that when we take pleasure, delight in the word of the Lord, and make it a part of our daily life, we shall be like a tree that is planted by the rivers of water (Psalm 1:2-3). Our marriage will be strong when we incorporate reading the Bible and following the instructions that God has given to us. Have you ever bought something that had to be put together and you put it together without the instructions? When you finished, it looked right, but later you had a problem and discovered that something was wrong, or you left something out. It was all because you chose not to read and follow the instructions that the manufacturer sent. Well, God has instructions, and when we choose not to follow them, we will have problems.

There is an answer for every situation in the Bible. There is nothing new that cannot be addressed from the word of God. Taking time to read the Bible and to apply the principles to your marriage is a sure way to make your marriage strong. It will be just like the tree that is planted by the rivers of water.

BOUNDARIES

Have you ever found yourself one-on-one with someone of the opposite sex and felt a little uncomfortable? How about being in an unexpected situation with someone of the opposite sex and you think, *This could be taken the wrong way if my spouse or someone else were to see me.*

Well, I have been in this type of situation twice in the eleven years that I have been married. One day after I had my first child, I was on maternity leave and planned to go to my job to have lunch with the people in my department. I had my baby with me. At this time there were two ladies and two men in my department. When I arrived, only one person was available, and it was one of the guys. I didn't have the courage to say, "Let's reschedule the lunch and go when everyone can make it." Since he was the only one available, and I didn't want him to think that I had anything against him, I went to lunch with this guy. On my way to the restaurant, the thought hit me, "You are a married woman going to lunch with someone of the opposite sex and bringing your baby. This does not look good."

I thought to myself, *He knows that I am married and with child and not the least bit interested in him.* In addition, he had never flirted with me or said anything to indicate that he was the least bit interested in me. Therefore, I wanted to feel that the lunch was okay; this was just a co-worker. However, I was not comfortable with this situation and vowed that I would never have a one-on-one meal with someone of the opposite sex. Sitting at the table with the opposite sex is intimate. I also thought, *If I were to see my husband in a restaurant having lunch with a woman, I know that I would not be pleased.* The Bible says, "Do unto others as you would have them to do unto you" (Matthew 7:12). After I thought about how I would feel if I saw my husband dining with another woman, I really felt bad. In order to release this, I had to confess it and discuss it with my husband. This happened early in our marriage; therefore, I took it as a lesson learned and vowed not to do that again. After discussing it, we started talking about our boundaries and vowed not to dine one-on-one with anyone of the opposite sex.

You may be thinking to yourself, what is the big deal? The big deal is that regular one-on-one dates with someone of the opposite sex could create problems in your marriage. It has happened so many times. Normally, affairs start with a casual phone call, dinner, lunch, or meeting. Many admit that the first time that they had the encounter with the opposite sex, it was not to have an affair. However, connecting with the opposite sex on a regular basis could initiate an affair. When you open the door for a member of the opposite sex to come into your world, watch out! One thing leads to another, and you could end up going further than you ever planned to go and staying longer than you ever planned to stay.

Therefore, boundaries are necessary. When longevity and happiness are a goal in your marriage, you need to have boundaries. What exactly are boundaries? *Webster's Dictionary* defines a *boundary* as something that indicates bounds or limits. Every married couple should establish and be able to communicate what the boundaries are. As I ask couples about their boundaries; many have assumed boundaries and have not actually talked about them. One young lady said that she had established boundaries in her head based on the way that she wanted to be treated. However, she and her husband had never had a conversation about the boundaries. Establishing boundaries can help to protect your relationship. There are people of the opposite sex who will try you just to see if you will go there.

The other situation that I encountered unexpectedly was when I went to an aromatherapy meeting. I know you are probably thinking, how could I go wrong there? The meeting started with all women in the room. Later, a gentleman came in and sat at the table where I was sitting along with several other women. First, there was a meeting about the possibilities of selling products, and then there was an aromatherapy session. There were about eight ladies in the session and then the gentleman walked in the room. I had a girlfriend sitting next to me, and there was an empty seat on the left of me. So guess who sat in the seat? The only gentleman who attended the session sat in the vacant seat next to me. During the session, we smelled all kinds of scents, and then the lady leading the session asked us to turn to the right and rub the shoulders of the person who was next to us. I didn't have a problem with this because it was my girlfriend. However, I was to the right of the gentleman, so he rubbed my shoulders. I thought to myself, this is not right, but I didn't have the courage to move or get up and walk out. I stayed, and a few minutes later, we were instructed to turn to the left and rub the person's shoulders who was next to us. So you guessed it, I rubbed his shoulders. One part of me thought, *I am in public, this is just an aromatherapy session, and my girlfriend is right here and can testify that there was nothing to it.* Even though there was nothing to it, it bothered me for the rest of the night. I thought, *How would I feel if William went to some session and rubbed some woman's shoulders?* I would not want that at all. Therefore, I knew that I was wrong. I beat myself over the head for not walking out of the room. However, I came home and, after thinking about it, I shared it with my husband. He was mad and upset that I allowed some other man to put his hands on me. He expressed that we should both have a boundary that says that no one of the opposite sex is to put their hands on us in such an intimate way. I apologized and vowed not to do that again. All it takes is a certain look, touch, or conversation, and that could be the start of a relationship outside of your marriage. Protect your marriage relationship by establishing boundaries, communicate them, and apply them. Here are some examples of common boundaries that we have set:

- We will not dine one-on-one with the opposite sex.
- We will not ride in a car with the opposite sex without making our spouse aware.
- We will not have regular conversations with anyone of the opposite sex via cell phone, telephone, or email.
- There will be no business trips or one-on-one meetings in private places with the opposite sex.

Be careful about what you allow to come into your eye gate. Sometimes, seeing certain things can trigger bad things. We have to be careful about the videos and visuals that we allow our eyes to see on a computer, the TV, or wherever. If these things stimulate desires or passions that do not include our wife or husband, they should be left alone. The enemy will slip in any way you allow him. This also applies to music. Different types of music can stimulate thoughts, desires, or passions that may not include your spouse. If so, this music should be left alone.

Now, some of these boundaries may sound a little extreme to you, but they work. The Bible says, "Make no room for the devil" (Ephesians 4:27) and "be not ignorant of his devices" (2 Corinthians 2:11). Sometimes, not having boundaries in one of these situations can lead to other problems in your marriage. Protect your marriage by establishing boundaries. Every marriage should establish boundaries!

CHAPTER THREE
THE *C* PRINCIPLES

CARE

Does your mate know that you care? Sometimes, we can get so busy with the cares of life that we forget to show each other that we care. As you express your concerns of the day, it is good to know that your mate is really listening and willing to alter his or her plans to show care. God cares for us (I Peter 5:7) and we need to show our care for each other.

One day, I had a full day; I had worked for eight hours and had a hair appointment right after work. My plan was to leave work and go straight to the hairdresser. In order for me to make my hair appointment on time, I couldn't make any stops. In the middle of the day, I mentioned to William that I had a busy evening and didn't know when I was going to eat because I didn't have time to stop to get anything. I didn't want to be late for my hair appointment. When I got off from work, I was hungry and my thought was, *I sure would like to have something to eat before I go to the hairdresser.* However, I didn't want to risk being late so I had just prepared myself to wait until later to eat.

When I got into the car after work, on the seat was a seafood salad, something to drink, and a note from my kids. William had gone to get me something to eat, so that I could have a meal before I went to the hairdresser, and Ciara wrote a note saying, "Thank you for helping me and Ahmad with our projects last night." This almost brought tears to my eyes. Why? William listened to my concerns about having to rush from work right to the hairdresser, not having any dinner. Not only did he hear me, he showed that he cared by going to get me something to eat, bringing it to my job, and placing it in the car so that it would be ready when I got off from work. Not only that, my children took the time to write me a thank you note because the night before, we worked hard to finish projects that both of them had for school. It means so much when your family takes time to show they care. Many times we say that we care, but we have to be intentional about showing that we care.

CELEBRATE

Making time to celebrate is essential to adding fun to your marriage relationship. This principle is all about observing special days and commemorating special events with ceremonies or festivities. In the book of Esther, the Jews celebrated special days with gladness, feasting, and sending presents to one another (Esther 9:19). Since life is short, we should look for opportunities to celebrate. It is a choice. You can choose to let special dates and milestones go by like it's nothing or you can find a way to celebrate.

I can remember when we first got married, we would celebrate the eighth day of every month. Our wedding day is August 8, so each time that we got to the eighth of the month, we would do something special. As time went on, after the first year, this eventually stopped. We had our first child a year later, and then we started celebrating other things, such as being pregnant, having a baby shower, giving birth, the christening, and then the baby's first birthday. Everything was centered around the baby. Most of us don't have problems celebrating things for our kids, but we take the back burner.

Life goes on, and it seems as if we find fewer reasons to celebrate each other. Well, I encourage you to find reasons to celebrate your husband or your wife. Celebrating doesn't always have to be done in a big and expensive way; it can be something as simple as having a candlelight dinner at home. It could be putting a special card in your spouse's car. It could be giving your mate a back rub, pedicure, or massage. Birthdays and anniversaries should always be celebrated, even if you can't do something big. Take time to celebrate. You could write a meaningful letter and just celebrate the fact that your spouse is still alive or that you are still married.

I recently celebrated my fortieth birthday and I really wanted to have a birthday party. I didn't expect one, because my husband is normally not one to plan events. A few months before my birthday, he asked me what I wanted and I told him. I really just wanted some friends and family around to help me celebrate my forty years of life. Well, I left the issue alone and decided that I would attend a conference the weekend of my birthday. I attended the conference from Friday to Saturday and returned home on Saturday evening. When I arrived home, my husband had given me a surprise birthday party. Many of my closest friends and family came together to help me celebrate. I couldn't believe that my husband pulled it off. In all of the years that we have been married, I have never seen him put together something of this magnitude. I was pleasantly surprised. Of course he had help from family and friends, but he did it! It made me feel so good to know that he put forth the effort. The whole idea of him planning something especially for me was thrilling!

Celebrations give us something to look forward to, and they add excitement to our days. Celebrations can be done with a little, a lot, or no money at all. It is all about taking time out to commemorate a special day, accomplishment, or just celebrating each other.

Every year our church sponsors a special event called "The Legacy of Love." The event is held during the week of Valentine's Day. Each year, my husband and I look forward to attending this event. We get all dressed up, and come together with hundreds of couples to celebrate the love that we have for each other. This year we attended and the Lord gave me a poem to share with couples about celebrating love.

Celebrate Love
by
Carolyn Tatem

Tonight we are here to celebrate love
Thanking God for marriage, a gift sent from above
Tonight we are here to celebrate love
At a time where couples are giving up, breaking up and divorcing
Tonight we are here to celebrate love
To have fun, dance and enjoy each other's company
Tonight we are here to celebrate love
Regardless of the ups, downs and the unexpected turn arounds
Tonight we are here to celebrate love
Communicate and stimulate your passion for one another
Tonight we are here to celebrate love
Choosing to forgive and allowing God to heal
Pushing all of your issues aside
Tonight we are here to celebrate love

Regardless of your finances
Let's rekindle the romance
Tonight we are here to celebrate love
When you feel like you have run out of love
Go to the One who is Love
As I Corinthians 13 says . . .
Love suffers long, and is kind
Love does not envy, it does not parade itself
Love is not puffed up, it does not behave rudely
Love does not seek its own, is not provoked,
Love thinks no evil, does not rejoice in iniquity,
But rejoices in the truth
Love bears all things, believes all things,
Hopes all things, endures all things,
Love never fails.

CLASSES

Have you ever taken a class with your mate? To be more specific, a class that helps to build your marriage, to increase intimacy, or just to have fun. My husband and I have taken several marriage-related courses over the years. Each course has helped me to learn something that perhaps I would not have learned. Sometimes, a class brings out information and behaviors that would have never come out in your everyday setting with your mate. Depending upon the class that you take, a class can help to stimulate conversation between you and your mate. It can also help to nourish and strengthen your marriage relationship. In addition, we have made new friends in each class. In most of the classes, couples have been transparent about their challenges. Sometimes, just hearing someone else's story is enough to help you appreciate your own marriage. Although every marriage has its challenges, we sometimes put too much focus on our own challenges. Taking a course with other couples can be a great eye-opener.

Another thing that I like about taking a class with my husband is that it forces us to really study on a consistent basis. Most of the courses lasted for several weeks. Each week, we would come together to do our homework and to study the lesson for the upcoming class.

You may be thinking that you don't have time to take a class together. I truly understand. My husband works four nights a week, and the only available weeknight that he has is Monday night. However, since building our marriage and helping to build other marriages has been a priority, we have signed up for courses on his only available night. It is always a sacrifice of our time and our time with our children. We have to find a babysitter, and we make time to take the class. When you see the class as vital to building and sustaining your marriage, you will make time.

Some couples take exercise courses together, ballroom dancing, or other physical activity classes. Each time, their marriage is strengthened. Take time out to take a class with your mate. It may be one of the best times that you have ever spent together.

COMMUNICATION

Many say that the key to a good marriage is communication. We hear this word so much, but what does it really mean? *Webster's Dictionary* says to *communicate* is to impart knowledge of, to make known, to transmit, to give or interchange thoughts and information. It also says it is to express one's true thoughts, feelings, and moods easily. It can be done in different ways, such as in person, by phone, in writing, or by sign language.

Usually, a relationship starts with some form of communication. It may be communicating by phone, in person, or on the computer. When we meet someone we are interested in knowing better, we will spend hours communicating to learn as much as we can. The more knowledge we get, the better we can determine if this is someone who we are interested in spending the rest of our life. It is usually the communication that stimulates us to continue the relationship. As the communication grows, the relationship grows, and for some, it leads to marriage. So, I would say that communication is the key that gets the marriage started. However, a lack of communication can be the key that ends the marriage.

Oftentimes, when the communication in a marriage relationship begins to die, the relationship will also die. I can remember in one of our first arguments, the first thing that I wanted to do was to stop talking to my husband. I just wanted to shut down and let him figure out what was wrong with me. When I began shutting down, the Lord began speaking to me. He said, "Carolyn, if you want to be married for any length of time, you must learn how to handle your disagreements."

I have learned that I may not feel like talking for the moment, but I must quickly come out of this mood and begin to communicate how I feel. It is not healthy to walk around without talking or holding in everything that you would like to say. When we express love the way that God would have us to, we cannot be rude or go around the house not talking. Yes, I agree, sometimes you don't need to say everything. However, you must learn to communicate even when things are not going your way. It is during these times that we learn more about each other. Communicating your feelings when you are hurt or upset helps your mate to learn more about you, and vice versa. Perhaps when your feelings are communicated, something will be learned that may prevent this situation from happening again.

A husband and wife must have some way of connecting in order to keep the relationship going strong. It is important that you communicate every day. The more that you communicate, the better the relationship can be. As we communicate our thoughts, ideas, moods, desires, and so on, we learn about our mates better. Learning about each other has a lot to do with how we communicate. The more that we learn about each other, the better we can understand each other. Understanding each other helps us to be able to meet each other's needs. Therefore, a lot of needs can be met based on our ability to communicate with each other.

There may be seasons in a marriage when a husband and wife cannot communicate every day due to the military or illness. In this case, one has to hold on to the memories until the communication can begin again. The good thing is that when the communication ends, it can be brought back to life. It just takes time to re-establish the communication process.

One of the most powerful scriptures to remember as you communicate is to: "Let no corrupt word proceed out of your mouth, but what is good for necessary edification, that it may impart grace to the hearers" (Ephesians 4:29). Before I say anything, I ask myself, "Is what I am about to say good? Does it edify?" If the answer is no, then I ask the Lord to help me to say something that would please Him.

COUCH TIME

The couch time principle is simply taking time out of your day to sit on the couch next to each other. My husband and I learned this principle from some friends before we got married. The rules are that you must take a few minutes out of each day to sit next to each other on the couch. There are two different ways that we use this principle. The first way that we use it is to communicate. The TV is turned off and there are no interruptions. We sit and talk about our day or anything that is on our mind. The second way that I use this principle is to get into my husband's world. He is a sports fan, so he frequently sits on the couch to watch sports. Usually, he is in the basement and I am upstairs. I am not interested in sports, so normally I don't bother him while he is watching a game. However, over the years, he has let me know that he would love my company while he is watching a game. So my goal has been to take out fifteen to thirty minutes to sit and watch a game with him. Each time that I do, it makes his day. I don't say much, I just sit and watch the game with him. We use this as a time to be physically close and to cuddle. I am often amazed by how it blesses him. He is a touchy, feely person, so when I sit next to him while he is watching the game, it gives him an opportunity to be touchy, feely. Sometimes, we are so busy living in the same house but in different worlds.

Sitting on the couch with my husband helps me to get into his world. It says, "I am interested in what you are interested in." It also says, "I want to be next to you." Taking time out of my evening schedule to sit down and watch a game that I am not interested in is not easy for me. However, since I know that it pleases my husband, I am learning to make it a priority. In the beginning, I saw this as a waste of time because I would be sitting and thinking about all of the things that I could be doing around the house, such as washing and folding the clothes, helping the kids with something, and so on. However, I recently have learned to see this time differently because it is important to my husband. Also, it has such a positive effect on him. Taking a few minutes out of my day to sit on the couch next to my husband has now become a priority, and I am learning to enjoy it. I encourage you to try it.

Perhaps your spouse is not a TV watcher. There may be something else that he or she enjoys doing. Whatever it is, I challenge you to get into your spouse's world. Observe and simply just practice being there. Be there to encourage, be there to support, and just be visible to say that you are interested in the same things. Don't let life get you so busy, wrapped up, and tangled up into the job, the house, the kids, and so on, that you don't take time to get into the things that your mate enjoys the most. Couch time is important!

CHAPTER FOUR
THE *D* PRINCIPLES

DATING

Why is it that married couples start out dating, but once they marry, dating becomes a thing of the past? Before we got married, we looked forward to getting all dressed up and going out to dinner, to the movies, or to someplace special. After we are married, dating our mates on a regular basis seems to be a thing of the past. It seems that once you are married, live together, pay bills, see each other's flaws, and have children, the desire to date is no longer as exciting as it used to be. However, dating is very important to keeping your marriage relationship healthy and fresh. We must fight for time to date our mates. Usually, the time will not just fall out of the sky. You must be intentional about spending regular, undisturbed time with your mate. It doesn't have to be an expensive date, it could just be going for a walk together. The key is having regular, one-on-one, undisturbed time together. The ideal goal is to have at least one day per week where you spend at least one to two hours (or more) together with your mate. I must admit that due to the demands of the week and having to find a babysitter, my husband and I have not consistently been able to keep our once-a-week date night. We are still working on this.

However, we do make it our business to have pillow talk at least once or twice per week. This is when we stay in the bed for thirty minutes or more, ask the kids to give us some time alone, and talk about whatever is on our mind. This gives us time to connect and to build intimacy. Couples who practice the principle of dating consistently during the marriage say that it has helped to keep them from divorcing. I encourage you to try something new together. A new place, a new restaurant, a new movie, and experience it together. When was the last time that you went out on a date with your mate? Make it happen.

DEVOTIONS

This principle is all about having a regular time where you and your mate come together to pray, read, and spend time in the presence of God. It could be for one minute or one hour. Any amount of time that you spend seeking God and His word will be beneficial to you, your mate, and your marriage. For whenever a husband and a wife are gathered together in the name of the Lord, He promises to be in the midst (Matthew 18:20). God is the one who created marriage. Therefore, each time that we go to Him, He has a way of strengthening our marriage relationship.

Some couples have daily devotions, some have weekly devotions, and some have it a few times a month. Whatever the time, you will be blessed when you take time out of your marriage to devote to the God who is able to do exceedingly, abundantly, above all that we can ask or think. We have made praying together as a couple and as a family a part of our daily routine. Our children have made praying and taking time to read their devotional book a part of their daily routine. The goal is to come to God together as a couple as often as you can. God will give you wisdom, direction, and strength to maintain and sustain you in your marriage.

There are various types of couples' devotional books that are very helpful. Normally, they have a topic for the day, a scripture and a passage to read. Most can be done in five to fifteen minutes. If you don't have a specific book to guide you, you can always read the Proverb of the day. There is a chapter in Proverbs that will match the day of the week. Read the chapter together and discuss the verse or verses that really speak to you. As a couple, you could also journal or write down your prayer concerns. As time goes on, you will be able to look back on what God has done in your marriage.

DISCIPLINE

Change requires discipline. If you want to change anything in yourself or in your marriage, you must use discipline.

Do you have the discipline to create a change? In August of 2008, I gained some unwanted weight. I put on an extra fifteen pounds. When my pants started getting too tight and I wasn't able to comfortably fit into my clothes, I decided that I had to make a change. I refused to go to the closet and not be able to wear something because I have gotten too big. I made up my mind that I must make a change. Most of us know when we need to make a change, but we don't have the discipline to do it. *Webster's Dictionary* defines *discipline* as "training to act in accordance with rules; instruction and exercise designed to train to proper conduct or action." Most people who are overweight know that they are overweight, they know that they need to make a change, but when it comes to eating differently and to exercising, they don't succeed. We often know what to do and know what it takes, but just can't bring ourselves to do it. Well, I decided to ask God for the discipline to eat right and to exercise on a regular basis. I looked at my schedule and decided I could make a change in the way that I started my day. The key was rising earlier to accomplish more with my time. Instead of getting up at 6:00 AM, I am up at 4:30 or 5:00 AM. By rising earlier, I am able to have time with the Lord through prayer, reading, and journaling. After my devotion time, I exercise for at least thirty minutes and then get my day started. I ask the Lord to help me to make better food choices each day. I love to eat, so eating right and eating smaller portions is a challenge. Any change that we are going to make will require discipline. In I Corinthians 9:27 Paul says that he had to discipline his body and bring it into subjection. Discipline yourself!

DIVORCE

In Malachi 2:16, the Lord God says that He hates divorce because it covers one's garment with violence. To divorce is to separate, disunion, to break the marriage contract between oneself, one's spouse, and God. When we first say our marriage vows, we often say that we will stay married until death we do part. The marriage covenant was never meant to be broken. Marriage is an institution created by God, and when a man and woman come together, He makes them one. So when God makes us one with our mates and we choose to divorce, there will be some major consequences.

The world that we live in makes divorce sound and appear so easy. Basically, the attitude of today is, if you get tired of dealing with each other and no longer want to handle the issues of your mate, get rid of him or her. The thought seems to be that God will understand; after all, He wants us to be at peace and to be happy. When we become a Christian, this means that we should be Christ like. If Jesus Christ lives in our hearts; how can we have peace with something that He hates? It breaks the heart of God. Divorce between two people who believe in a mighty God is like saying that our God is not powerful enough to make our marriage work. It says that we didn't want to wait long enough to see God turn the marriage around; we got tired of waiting on the change, so we said, "The heck with it! Let's separate." Oftentimes, the separation takes place without really considering ALL of the damage that will be done and ALL of the people who will be hurt. It is not just about you and your happiness. You see, most of us have weddings and invite witnesses to the wedding. Divorce hurts all of the witnesses who later find out that we are divorced, as well as any children who may have come out of the marriage. Divorce makes our children vulnerable. In verse 15 of the second chapter of Malachi, God says that He wants us to have a godly offspring. The devil's job is to steal, kill, and destroy (John 10:10) by any means necessary. When he gets parents to divorce, it makes it so much easier for him to get to the children. Parents are the covering that God intended to protect the children. When the marriage covenant is broken, our children will suffer. A husband and wife who separate or divorce can open the door for many other things.

As humans, we want to make divorce a light thing, but it is not. The scripture says that it covers one's garments with violence (Malachi 2:16). I have never heard anyone elaborate on this. Why would the word of God choose to relate the word *violence* with divorce? Violence can be defined as characterized by or arising from injurious or destructive forces. When a divorce takes place, people are hurt. I believe that when God joins a man and woman together, He makes them one. Imagine one body, and then imagine part of that body being cut into half. That one body is now injured, and because of the injury, there will be some pain. When a man and woman are joined together in the institution called marriage, God's desire is that they rely on, depend on, and access Him on a daily basis. Including God in the marriage will be the glue that holds it together. Excluding God from the marriage will be the very thing that tears a marriage apart. God has the power to heal, change, redirect, and restore any relationship. Will you let Him do it?

CHAPTER FIVE
THE *E* PRINCIPLES

EATING

When we first got married, my husband made a request. His request was that he would like for us to eat all of our meals at the kitchen table. Although I didn't grow up eating every meal at the table, I had no problem with the request. I thought it was a great idea; I didn't know that it was a God idea. Later in our marriage, I learned about the biblical significance of eating at the table. The measurements for the table were given in the Bible (Exodus 25:8-9, 23-30), and the purpose of the table was to bring people together and, most importantly, to have the presence of Jesus at the table. In Revelation 3:20, He states, "Behold! I stand at the door and knock. If anyone hears My voice and opens the door, I will come in to him and dine with him, and he with Me." Jesus wants to dine with us at the table. It is a trick of the enemy to have us so busy and our families so separated that we don't ever come together to eat at the table.

I have learned that there are so many blessings in eating together at a table, especially when you have children. In my experience, I get to look everyone in the eye at the table. I also learn about everyone's day at the table. If there is something wrong with my husband or my children, I can usually detect it at the table. Cooking a meal and eating at the table allows me the opportunity to nurture my family in more ways than one. They are nurtured not only physically, but mentally and spiritually. The meal nurtures them physically. The communication, encouragement, and sometimes a scripture is shared to nurture them mentally and spiritually. There is power in eating at the table together as a family.

Today, many of our lives are so busy that we are not taking the time to cook or sit down and have meals together. When we don't come together on a regular basis, we are likely to miss something significant that God wants to reveal about our mate or our children. However, each time that we do dine together, we become more in tune (see the In Tune Principle) with our family, and relationships are strengthened. Dining together should be so routine that our family looks forward to meeting at the table. Other traditions can be added to the table, like sharing a scripture, inviting a guest to the table, making special meals and recipes. Jesus wants to meet our families at the table.

Now, if you would like to implement this principle, it may take some time if everyone is not used to being home around the same time. Ideally, it is great if you can start this principle at the beginning of your marriage and continue it even after having children. This way, everyone will have made it a habit. However, if it is new to your family, you may want to start by having a family meeting and explaining the significance of having everyone dine at the table together. Also, share the fact that Jesus wants to meet us at the table. There are so many things that He wants to reveal to us about our families while we are at the table.

ENCOURAGE

When it comes to doing something for the first time, I have a tendency to be nervous or second-guess whether I can do it. I can think of so many times that I have been apprehensive and God used my husband to come along and give me the encouragement that I needed to move forward.

He has been my biggest cheerleader for writing this book. I have been writing for a couple of years and I would probably still be writing. However, William kept encouraging me to finish. A few months ago, he asked, "What can I do to help you?" I said it would be nice if I had a laptop computer. I would be able to get up and write without getting out of the bed. I know this is lazy of me. However, sometimes the thought of getting up and going downstairs to write was not motivating. About two weeks later, William and the kids surprised me by giving me a laptop. I was so encouraged because he wanted to do whatever he could do to help me get the job done. Sometimes, he blesses me by just giving me time to write; as a result, this book is finished.

I was a stay-at-home mom for six years and decided to go back to teaching so that I could teach at the school where my children attend. I knew that eventually I would have to renew my certification so that my teaching license would be in good standing. The thought of having to return to college after being out for over ten years was not appealing to me. But William encouraged me all of the way. He prayed for me and with me. In addition, he made sure that our children were taken care of while I was busy with school work. Our children understood that Mommy had to go to school and study and that this was temporary. Having the encouragement and support of my family meant the world to me. I was able to take the courses that I needed and renew my teaching license.

When I was first asked to lead a ministry in our church, fear came over me. I was okay with helping someone else lead, but I was afraid to be the one in the forefront. I didn't want the responsibility, so my initial response was to say, "No, thank you. I will help someone else, but I am not interested in leading." William encouraged me to give it a try. He said that God had already prepared me and equipped me with everything that I need to be a good leader. I accepted the leadership responsibility over three years ago, and each year, the Lord has been faithful at helping me to carry out the role as director of the Queen Esther Ministry (a ministry that teaches young women).

As decisions come my way, I have learned to share them with my husband. God uses him to give me direction, confidence, and encouragement to do things that I would not have done on my own.

ENDURE

In 1 Corinthians 13:7 it says that love endures *all* things. If everyone practiced what this principle says, there would be no reason to exit a marriage. The word that doesn't allow any excuses is *all*. When we have the love of God in our marriage, He helps us to endure. To endure is to hang in there without giving up, to go through great pain or pressure and still hang in there, to bear without resistance or with patience, to tolerate, or to last. Now there is no way that we can successfully do this by ourselves. We need the power of God to help us, because sometimes we are faced with some difficult situations in our marriage. When we are mistreated, cheated on, lied to, abused, misused, and so on, our natural inclination is often to quit. No one wants to endure when things aren't going well. In our weakness, God's grace is sufficient. He has the power to change a person's heart, and because of that, we can endure.

ENTERTAINING

This principle is about inviting guests into your home and showing them hospitality. Your home is an extension of yourself. When we invite guests into our home, we learn more about our friends and they learn more about us. Sometimes our friends invite their friends to our home and we get to meet new people. The Bible encourages us to entertain guests and to be given to hospitality (Romans 12:12 and Hebrews 13:2). Our homes should be a place where we are comfortable inviting others in and not be ashamed. Some people are so private that they wouldn't dream of entertaining. God created us for fellowship, and He certainly likes when we share what we have with others. When we invite guests into our home, prepare a meal, and sit at a table to break bread, God will be in our midst. His presence is at the table. This means that we should do a good job of maintaining a decent home. One reason that people don't like to entertain is that their home is not clean or ready to receive guests. This means that as the days go by, we should maintain our homes to a level that we could entertain at any time. I admit that sometimes my house is cleaner than others. When I know that I am having guests, I put a special touch on everything. I do have young children, and I am still learning and teaching them to put things back where they belong so that we can all help to maintain a neat and clean house. It is not easy. However, entertaining on a regular basis motivates me to maintain a clean house. Are you ready to entertain?

CHAPTER SIX
THE *F* PRINCIPLES

FAITHFUL

Can you be faithful to the bride or the groom of your choice? I have seen so many relationships damaged because someone chooses to be unfaithful. When a man and a woman make a decision to get married, they make a vow before God to be faithful. God is the key to helping every man and woman to keep and honor their wedding vows.

There will always be someone who looks better, dresses better, has a better job, and maybe even treats you better than the one you selected for marriage; however, if you start paying close attention to that someone, you may find yourself being unfaithful.

The Bible is very clear on the need for a husband and a wife to be faithful. In Proverbs Chapter 5 verses 15-20 we are told to "Drink water from your own cistern, And running water from your own well." As I researched this verse, I found that a cistern is a reservoir or a tank for storing water. This verse is used to refer to intercourse within marriage and enjoying the spouse that God has given to you. The word tells us to make sure that you are getting intercourse from your own well. In the Old Testament times water was a precious commodity. When a family had a well, it was their most important possession. It was a crime to steal water from someone else's well. In comparison, it is a crime to have intercourse with another man's wife or a another women's husband. In verse 18 and 19 the passage tells a husband to rejoice with the wife of his youth and to "Let her breasts satisfy you at all times, And always be enraptured with her love." God designed for a husband and wife to enjoy each other and to be so satisfied that there is no need to go outside of the marriage.

To be faithful is to honor and respect your mate so much that you will not violate the relationship with someone else. Too many marriages and families have been broken because someone decided to sexually violate their marriage relationship. The pain and damage that comes with unfaithfulness is so great that it is difficult to move forward. Often times, it hurts the entire family. Therefore, choose to be faithful. Know that the Lord our God is faithful and He empowers us to be faithful to our mate (Deuteronomy 7:9).

FINANCES

One of the most challenging areas in my marriage has been finances. Two people coming together from different backgrounds and different beliefs about money and how it should be managed makes handling finances difficult. I don't think that either one of us came from backgrounds where we were really taught how to properly manage money. So we have learned by trial and error over the last eleven years of our marriage. Perhaps you can learn from some of our mistakes. We have learned some valuable lessons as it relates to finances. I will share the ones that stand out to me most.

The first lesson that we learned was that our money should be joined together. Having your money in one account requires trust and communication. You have to trust God that your mate will do what is supposed to be done with the money. You must communicate so that you are clear on how the money will be managed. One of the hardest things for us was communicating about our ATM cards. I would use the card to take money out, William would use the card to take money out, and if we did not communicate, our account would have less than we expected. There were times when we had checks written and we didn't communicate on what we were taking out, so the check bounced because we did not talk about the money we spent. Having a check bounce was humiliating for me, so we worked really hard to get better in this area. We ended up having an account specifically for paying bills. So we only paid bills from this account; we did not use the ATM card or take money out.

The second lesson was to decide who will be the one to pay the bills. I used to think that the man should be the one to pay the bills. However, if he is not good at keeping records and paying the bills on time, then this shouldn't be his job. Whoever is best with the finances should be the one to pay the bills. It is important that you communicate and have a written record or budget each time that the bills are paid so that you both are clear on how the money was managed.

The third lesson that we learned was to not make quick decisions when it comes to how money is going to be spent. We have been in situations where something was presented to us that required a deposit or a financial commitment, and because it sounded good, we went for it. We didn't take enough time to pray or to process how the decision would affect our household. So don't allow someone to put you in a corner and say you have to purchase today or this is the only day that you will be able to get this deal. I have listened to some persuasive salespeople and made some poor decisions.

The fourth lesson was to create a budget. No matter who does the bills, both of you should be aware of everything coming in and everything going out. There should be boundaries and guidelines on what you spend and save. A budget will help to keep you in line.

The fifth lesson was to keep good records. I can't tell you the number of times that we have needed to find a record of something related to the finances. If you have a filing system and keep everything organized, it will make life easier for you later.

FORGIVENESS

One day I was teaching an eighth grade class with nineteen students. I would begin class by playing music on my iPod for the first five minutes. I believe that music can set the tone for the class as students are entering the room. I would play the music while students were working on a warmup assignment. After the warmup, I turned the music off and began teaching class. The class was about fifty minutes long. When class was dismissed, the students proceeded to exit and another class was waiting to come in.

I turned my back toward my desk and the table where my iPod was and proceeded to greet the next group of students who were entering the class. As I went to the door to greet them, never leaving my classroom, I thought, *Let me turn the music on for the next class.* I turned around to walk back to the table where my iPod was, but it was gone. Yes! It was gone. I could not believe it; one of the students had stolen my iPod. I started looking all over the class but it was gone. I immediately went to get the class who had just left the classroom and asked them to come back to the room. I asked everyone, "Where is my iPod? It was in the room when the eighth grade class entered and was gone when the eighth grade class exited. What happened? Who took my iPod?"

No one admitted to seeing or doing anything. I was in a state of shock. I couldn't believe that this was happening. I couldn't believe that a student in the eighth grade class could be so bold. The thought of a student stealing from their teacher while the teacher was in the room was horrible. It hurt me. Only God knew who took this iPod.

I began to pray for the student who took my iPod, and I asked others to pray. I prayed that God would change their heart and that it would be returned. Meanwhile, I had to deal with continuing to teach this class, not knowing which one of the students stole from me. I had to look each one in the eye and treat them just as if it had not happened. In my own strength, this is tough because in the back of my mind, I often thought, *Which one of you stole my iPod?* However, a few days after this happened, the Lord began to speak to me about my thoughts.

Matthew 6:14 says that I am to forgive men of their trespasses, meaning the wrong that they have done to me. In addition, if I don't forgive men of their trespasses, the Lord will not forgive me. Therefore, forgiveness is a choice. I could choose to continue to be hurt, hold a grudge against the class, and treat them differently, or I could choose to forgive, be kind, and rest in the fact that God will take care of the student who stole the iPod.

The valuable lesson that I learned from this situation relates so well to marriage. A key ingredient for longevity in marriage is practicing forgiveness. God is a forgiving God. He gives us the power to forgive; however, forgiveness is a choice. We can choose to be angry and constantly bring the trespass up over and over, or we can forgive. Forgiving doesn't always mean that you will forget; however, I have learned that you have to act like you have forgotten so that you don't keep dwelling on it in your mind. Also, you don't want to keep bringing the hurt or the sin up over and over. God will deal with the person who has wronged you. Through the power of God, we can demonstrate forgiveness to the person who has harmed us.

We must remember that we do wrong and sin every day, and we want God to forgive us. Therefore, we must forgive others, and this includes our mate. Imagine God constantly reminding us of our wrong and treating us differently because we have sinned. Anyone can be kind to those who are kind to them. However, a real test of our relationship with God is when we can love and be kind to someone who has wronged or hurt us. God is love. We must go to God on a regular basis to get love and then to give love to the person who has wronged us. Is this easy? No, it is not, but with God, all things are possible. God wants us to forgive, so He gives us power to forgive. We must choose to forgive. Forgive your husband or your wife, and ask God to give you a love and kindness toward your mate. God will do it!

FRIENDSHIP

Imagine getting married and having a child with a major illness. Imagine having a child who dies. Imagine going through a season where there is little or no income coming in and you are not sure how you are going to make ends meat. Would your marriage be able to survive these storms? Well, one of the secrets to surviving in a marital storm is having a solid friendship and being a good friend. Proverbs 17:17 says that a friend loves at all times.

Friendship is being intimate with your mate, having a sense of harmony and a safe place. Being able to be yourself and share your innermost thoughts without being criticized is a key to a successful friendship. I have heard so many couples say that if they didn't have a good friendship, their marriage would not have survived.

So how do you develop a good friendship? You let each other know that you can communicate without holding back. Create a safe place by not attacking your mate when he or she shares his or her feelings. Learn to respect each other's feelings, even when you don't agree. Recognize that if your mate feels a certain way, there is a reason. Make it your business to spend regular time getting to know each other better and having fun together. You need to be able to share without being afraid of the consequences. Sharing without your mate taking it personally or without your words being used against you at another time is important to establishing a good friendship. Sometimes, friendship is just listening or being there.

As a wife, I always want to provide a safe place for William to come. I would hate to think that he had something heavy on his mind and didn't feel comfortable enough to share it with me because of my reactions. We are best friends because we spend a lot time talking and sharing. We have continued to date each other, laugh, and have fun together. We both enjoy some of the same things together. I am thankful that I feel comfortable sharing my innermost thoughts and feelings. Communication is the key to developing a good friendship with your mate.

CHAPTER SEVEN
THE *G* PRINCIPLES

GIVE

Before William and I were married, God gave us a passion to help other couples. We were engaged and seeking to learn as much as we could about marriage God's way. We had dinner with a lot of different couples and were able to learn something from each. After we were married, we made a commitment to always do something to help other couples. A few years after being married, we started having get-togethers for engaged and newlywed couples. We would pick a topic that we thought that couples would benefit from, such as intimacy, finances, or communication. Each couple would bring a dish, and we would have a good time sharing and discussing the topic. The purpose of each fellowship was to help strengthen and encourage the institution of marriage.

William and I have been faithfully hosting a newlywed fellowship in our home every month (except August, our vacation month) for the past seven years. Sometimes, we facilitate a marriage class at our church. We are committed to giving of ourselves in this way. The more that we give to other couples, the more that our marriage is blessed. We have learned so much by helping and giving to other couples. Whatever we learn, we share it with other couples. Even when you think you don't have anything to give, there is always a lesson. Giving in a transparent way can help to strengthen someone else's marriage. Take time to give to someone else. Sharing your stories and experiences, and giving of yourself can make a big difference. Give and it shall be given back to you (Luke 6:38).

GOALS

Every January, I pull out my journal and start talking to my husband about what he wants to accomplish during the year. We discuss where we are and where we would like to be. It's not always a comfortable conversation, because sometimes we don't like looking at where we are and the changes that we need to make in order to get to where we want to be.

However, I think that it so important that we ask questions like what do we want to accomplish this year? What changes can we make to help us get to our goal? What is the time frame that we would like to accomplish this goal? We both know that we can only accomplish the goal with God's help. When we communicate the goals, I write them down and begin praying about the things that we have written down. If it is God's will, I trust Him to orchestrate the events of our days so that we can accomplish the goals. Oftentimes, it is not a lot of things, usually not more than five. Some of the goals are individual, and some are goals that we need to work together to accomplish. However, the goals usually require discipline in order for us to accomplish them.

Sharing our goals helps us to better understand each other and allows us the opportunity to support each other. At the end of the year, we can go back to the journal and check off what God has done through us and for us. Goals give us something to aim for; what are your goals? Have you written them down and shared them with your mate? Set some goals! If you don't aim for something, you will fall for anything.

GOD

Since marriage is an institution that God created, it was never meant to be maintained without God. Ecclesiastes 4:12 says that a threefold cord is not easily broken. I imagine a cord with three strands. One strand represents God. The second strand represents the husband, and the third strand represents the wife. The strands are so tightly knitted together that they cannot easily be broken. God desires to be the glue that keeps the marriage together. However, we must include Him in our everyday life. We should make Him a part of our marriage through reading, praying, going to church on a regular basis, and most importantly, being obedient to what the word says. So many people read, pray, and go to church, but they do not live out the principles of God in their marriage.

Oftentimes, when serious problems arise in our marriage, it is because we have neglected a part of the threefold cord. We must be mindful of God and do what His word says to do. God wants our marriage to be a reflection of Him. When God is in the midst of our marriage, He makes our marriage so attractive. Others can see that there is something different. God brings a harmony and a shine, which brings glory and honor to Him. This doesn't mean that your marriage is perfect; it simply means that God shines over any problem or difficulty that may be taking place in your marriage.

GODLY SEEDS

Did you know that God loves when we have children? Genesis 1:22 says, "Be fruitful and multiply." Children are gifts from God. However, when He gives us the gift, there is something that He wants us to do with it. It is not just having child after child after child that excites God. God seeks a godly offspring (Malachi 2:15). He gets excited when we reproduce children who have a heart and a love for Him.

Oftentimes, parents spend so much time making a living and doing other things that parenting is neglected. Every moment that we get to spend with the precious gifts that God blesses us with should be treasured. Deuteronomy 6:6–7 says, "These words which I command you today shall be in your heart. You shall teach them diligently to your children, and shall talk of them when you sit in your house, when you walk by the way, when you lie down, and when you rise up." This means that we should always be teaching our children and preparing them to be a godly seed.

The most powerful way to raise a godly seed is to live a godly life. Children are very observant. They notice everything. They hear what we say and see what we do. They know when we are for real and when we are being fake. They observe how we are in church and then how we live when we are at home. Living by example is one of the best ways to raise a godly seed. Our relationship with our mate is constantly observed by our children. They see behind the closed doors, and they know when Mom and Dad really love each other. If Mom and Dad are not demonstrating a loving relationship, then the children will be affected in some way. Each day, we must take advantage of the opportunity to pour into our children. We should be prepared to pour in God's word on a regular basis. Let's raise a godly seed.

CHAPTER EIGHT
THE *H* PRINCIPLES

HEALTH

Having good health is something that I think we often take for granted in our marriage. It is so important to enjoy your mate while you have health. I know that God is the giver of life, and He determines when our time on earth is done. However, while we are here, there are some things that we can do to stimulate good health.

Having our health means being able to walk, talk, move, and breathe without the use of a machine or someone helping us to get around. It also means doing things that we know are good for our bodies and not doing things that are harmful like using drugs, smoking, and drinking. What we put in our bodies has a lot to do with the quality of life that we have.

If you live long enough, there may come a day where you can't get around the way that you used to. I love when I see couples who have been married for thirty-plus years and they still look good. Oftentimes, when you talk to them, they have made some choices in reference to taking care of their health that have helped to make the difference. As we get older, our bodies change and they don't function the same way that they did in our younger years.

It is so important for us to take care of our physical bodies so that we can have better health. Resting, eating right, exercising, and taking care of our bodies will allow us to enjoy a better quality of life. We must encourage each other to make regular visits to the doctor to see about our bodies. If we don't take care of our bodies, it will create poor health. In the Third Book of John, verse two, he prays that you may prosper in all things and be in health, just as your soul prospers. In marriage, we must take care of our bodies and take care of each other. If we don't have our health, we will not be able to enjoy anything.

HELPER

"And the Lord God said, 'It is not good for man to be alone, I will make him a helper comparable to him'" (Genesis 2:18). Whenever I think about a helper, I think about a computer class that I used to teach. After the students had been coming to class for a period of time, I would observe the students who were struggling. Some students would let you know that they needed help, but with others, you just had to figure out that they were struggling. Well, after observing the students who knew the software really well and observing the ones who did not, I came up with an idea. I decided to put the students who were thriving and doing a great job with a student who was struggling. The student who knew the software well would be right there to assist the student who was struggling. So in other words, the students who were having challenges were placed with those who were not. They were positioned side by side so that the student who was doing well would be able to help the student who was not doing well. After a while, the student who was struggling would learn from his or her neighbor and begin to get the swing of the software.

I think this situation is what God had in mind when He created a woman. The first woman in the Bible is described as a helper who is comparable to her man. God created the wife to be a helper because He knew that husbands would need some help. In fact, we all need help at some point. A man can be just as helpful to his wife. The question that we should ask God is, "How can I help my spouse get to the place that you have just for him or her?" This is another reason why spending time with the Lord on a daily basis is important. As you spend time with God, He will deposit wisdom and ways that you can better help your spouse. It may be something that you need to say or do that helps your spouse develop into a fine man or woman of God. In 1 Peter 3:1 it says that a man can be won by the conduct of his wife. It also says that when our husbands observe our chaste conduct, and the respect that we have for God, they will be helped. What is your conduct like? Are you helping your man or hurting him?

HONEY

When I was growing up, I remember my former pastor telling married people to "keep the honey in the moon." I am not sure where he got the saying from; it may have been an original. However, honey is something sweet, delicious, or delightful. The moon represents marriage. Just by hearing this saying, I learned at an early age that marriage can sometimes get sour. It is up to the husband and the wife to do something to keep the honey in the marriage.

Honey may mean doing something extra nice to surprise your spouse or to let them know that you love them. Honey may mean taking a weekend getaway to change your scenery. Honey may mean buying flowers and giving them to your spouse. It could also mean giving a back or hand massage. Whenever we make a special effort to do something for our mate that is out of the everyday routine, we stir up honey in the moon. Honey is just taking the time to be sweet.

Honey is delicious; it may mean fixing your spouse's favorite meal or taking time to purchase something that your spouse would enjoy eating. William likes carrot cake, and there is a restaurant that makes the best carrot cakes. Occasionally, when I am near the restaurant, I will surprise him and bring a slice (big slice) of carrot cake home. Doing things like this says, "I was thinking of you while I was out."

Honey is delightful! This is when you give great pleasure, satisfaction, and enjoyment to your spouse. Every husband and wife should know and learn how to be delightful to their mate. Learn what it takes to satisfy and highly please your mate. As a wife, it is important to learn what satisfies and pleases your husband. When you learn what it takes, aim to please. This is so delightful! It is also important that a husband does the same for his wife.

Do you have honey in your moon? If not, it is not too late. It is just a matter of coming up with a way to be extra sweet, delicious, or delightful. You can do it. Surprise your mate, do something different that you know will please your mate. Keep the honey in the moon.

HOUSEWORK

It doesn't matter if you live in an apartment, condominium, townhouse, or single-family house, wherever you lay your head will require some housework. It is no fun to come home to a nasty and messy house. Maintaining a clean house is essential for creating a healthy environment to nourish your marriage. If the house is always in a mess with clutter everywhere, this can build tension in your marriage that doesn't have to be there. The home environment needs to be maintained on a regular basis.

In Titus 2:4 women are admonished to be homemakers. This means that women are responsible for making the house a home and managing the home. This doesn't mean that she has to keep the house clean all by herself. Having help from her husband and her children makes the job easier.

Each couple needs to decide who will be the one to keep the house clean. Will they hire someone? Will they split the chores, or will the person who prefers to do the cleaning be totally responsible and the other do something else? Each household is different. The important thing is that the house is maintained. In our house, I do most of the inside chores, and William does all of the outside chores, such as taking the trash out, mowing the lawn, trimming the hedges, washing the cars, and so on. He also helps with a few indoor chores like vacuuming, cooking, washing the dishes, and helping with the laundry. He doesn't do things the same way that I would do them, but I have learned to celebrate the fact that he helps. I don't complain, because complaining may cause him to never help in that area again.

The goal is to keep the house running in such a way that promotes a healthy marriage relationship. Housework is something that should be shared in some way, because it is no fun for one person to have to do everything when both are living in the same house. Helping each other to maintain a clean and neat house should be a common goal. Both of you have to be willing to give of yourselves and your time to maintain the housework.

CHAPTER NINE
THE *I* PRINCIPLES

IN TUNE

There have been some days where I have come home and greeted my husband and sensed that something isn't right. He says that he is doing okay and everything seems okay on the outside, but I still sense that something is wrong. It's hard to explain but when the two become one, you are connected. So if one part of you is hurt or affected in some way, you feel it. The more time that you spend together as husband and wife, you bond and become in tune with each other.

Being in tune is being in agreement and on one accord with your mate. There is a harmony, peace, concurrence in attitudes and in feelings. I have said all of this to show that there have been some days where something is going on with William, and for whatever reason, he is not ready to share it. However, because we are one and in tune with each other, I can pick up on the fact that something is not right with him. When this happens, I begin to pray and ask William questions to see if he wants to talk about it. One day, someone had stolen something out of his work truck. It made him mad but he hadn't discussed it with me. He just kept it to himself until I inquired. I could see that something was bothering him.

So there will be times when your mate may not vocalize a problem or something that is bothering them. When we are in tune with each other, God gives us the ability to discern and sense when something is not right. It may not ever be said, but when we experience this, we need to talk to God. He knows everything there is to know about us, and oftentimes, He will reveal it. When you pray, ask God to give you direction on how to handle what you are sensing. This may be a time where you have to initiate asking questions to encourage your mate to discuss whatever's bothering them.

INITIATE

One of the things that seems to make my husband happy each time is when I initiate making love to him. It makes his day! He thanks me a couple of times and he thanks God. He is so appreciative of me pursuing him in bed. Everyone needs to feel wanted, and although he knows that I want him, he says that it means so much when I show him in this way. The husband shouldn't be the only one initiating; this should work both ways. So if you are not the one who usually starts the love making, remember that your mate desires to be pursued. I have heard several men say, "I want my wife to come on to me for a change." Although I don't always reach this goal, my goal is to initiate at least once a week.

Now in order for me to reach my goal, I have to start thinking about making love to my husband before it's time to go to bed. I begin to plan what I am going to wear to bed (or whether I am going to wear anything at all). And I have to prepare my mind to initiate. Preparing my mind is important because I have found that I can quickly start thinking about a million other things that I need to do, the kids, or just how tired I am. I begin to focus my mind on my husband, how much of a blessing it is to have a husband, and how happy I know that it makes him feel when I initiate. Have you initiated lately?

INTIMACY

When I think of intimacy, I think of closeness, knowing each other, and understanding each other. Some automatically think of sex. However, I believe that intimacy goes so much deeper. The actual act of sex is intimate, but in this world that we live in, so many experience the intimate act of sex without ever becoming intimate. Some lay down without knowing some of the basics about the other person. God designed the husband and wife to be intimate companions. In the Book of Ecclesiastes, the value of having a mate is explained. Ecclesiastes 4:9–12 says, "Two are better than one, because they have a good reward for their labor. For if they fall, one will lift up his companion. But woe to him who is alone when he falls, for he has no one to help him up." Again, if two lie down together, they will keep warm; but how can one be warm alone? Though one may be overpowered by another, two can withstand him. And a threefold cord is not quickly broken."

This verse lets us know several things: 1) It is a blessing to be married and have a mate, because two are better than one. I know that sometimes the relationship can be so hard that you feel like you would be better off by yourself. However, the second part of the verse encourages you to hang in there because of the next benefit: 2) You will have a good reward for your labor. When I think of labor, I think of hard work. God is saying that the two are better than one and that if we hang in there, we will have a good reward for the hard work that we are doing in our marriage. 3) The third benefit is that if one falls, the other is there to lift up his or her mate. Where you are weak, perhaps your mate is strong. God intended for you to be able to lift your mate up. Intimacy with your mate helps to relieve loneliness and isolation. When a husband and wife are intimate, they are better able to comfort, assist, and defend each other. The scripture says that if you are alone, you will not have a physical body to help. 4) The fourth benefit is that the two can lie down together and help to keep each other warm. How intimate is that! I have experienced being in bed by myself, under the covers and freezing. However, when my husband gets in the bed and lies next to me or even touches me, my body begins to get warm. God designed the body to be able to warm another body. 5) The last part of the verse mentions a threefold cord that is not quickly broken. The deeper the intimacy between a husband and wife, the harder it is for the marriage relationship to be broken. Where there is no intimacy, there is loneliness and isolation. Isolation soon leads to separation, and separation leads to divorce. Intimacy is a key ingredient to a healthy marriage.

How is intimacy obtained? Intimacy is developed over time, time that is used to communicate, share, and learn about each other as the years go by. We should never feel like we know everything there is to know about our mate, because there is always something that we can learn. Study your mate; spend time with your mate; ask questions; spend time listening, observing, and allowing God to draw you closer. Pray and ask God to make you more intimate with your mate.

ISOLATION

Eric and Tracey have been married for a few years (true story, names are changed). Eric is no longer happy about being married. Things are not the way that he thought they would be. In addition, he is going through some issues on his job. He has discussed some of the issues with Tracey, but as time goes on, he begins to shut down. He doesn't have much to say to Tracey when she gets home. Eric goes downstairs to the basement and Tracey spends her time upstairs. He no longer wants to go out and do anything together. Therefore, Tracey says that she has started looking for things that she can do alone or with one of her girlfriends. There is nothing much happening in the bedroom because of the distance that they are experiencing. Tracey would like to reach out to someone to get some counseling, but Eric is not interested. He claims that there is nothing wrong with him or their marriage. Eric has embraced isolation. Tracey feels stuck because she doesn't feel like she can talk to anyone, so she tries to deal with this. Her way of coping is learning to do things by herself or with one of her girlfriends.

In one of the marriage courses that William and I took, we learned a formula which said that Isolation + Separation = Divorce. The message behind the formula is when husbands and wives get to the point that they don't want to be bothered with each other, they have a tendency to stop being around each other. They go into isolation. They don't want to spend time together; they want to be alone or just don't want to be with their spouse. When this attitude continues, it leads to separation. Separation is getting to the point where you decide to physically go your separate ways, since there is no togetherness. Once there is a separation, unless something is being done to reconcile, it is very likely that the separation will lead to divorce.

Who wants to get married and spend all of your time apart? One of the purposes of marriage is companionship. So if you get married and your spouse no longer wants to spend time together, it can lead to separation and then to divorce.

CHAPTER TEN
THE *J* PRINCIPLES

JESUS

At the age of twelve, my grandmother took me to church and I was introduced to Jesus Christ. I learned that we all have sinned and we all come short, so we all are in need of a Savior. Jesus Christ died, was buried, and rose again just for me. At the age of twelve, I made a decision to accept Jesus Christ as my personal savior. For Romans 10:13 says whoever calls on the name of the Lord shall be saved. Once I made this decision, I learned that Jesus Christ lived within me and it was up to me to cultivate this new relationship. I learned to cultivate my relationship with Jesus Christ through prayer, reading the Bible, going to church, and applying everything that I learned to my daily life. As my relationship with Jesus Christ began to grow, I became a new person. My walk changed, my talk changed, and my desires changed at the age of twelve. I really enjoyed having an intimate walk with the Lord; therefore, I continued my walk through junior high school, high school, college, graduate school, and even until today. Having a relationship with Jesus Christ is the best thing that has ever happened to me. I love the Lord so much that I want all of my ways to please Him.

As I began praying for a husband, I prayed that the Lord would give me a man who loved Jesus Christ and who would love the ground that I walked on. You see, my biological father never wanted to accept me as his child. He denied me for many years and came into my life at the age of nineteen. We maintained contact for a few years, and then he walked completely out of my life. I have tried to re-establish contact, but have been unsuccessful. It has been over ten years since I have seen or spoken to him. This is not by my choice. I would love to have a relationship with my father. However, he has chosen not to connect with me. Therefore, when I learned that I could have a relationship with Jesus Christ, and He is a Father who would never leave me nor forsake me, I was sold. Jesus has been the best Father that I could ever have. I have never wanted or needed anything that Jesus Christ didn't provide. I wanted to have a husband who would love Jesus and love me. I knew that in order for him to give me the love that I needed, he would need to have a relationship with Jesus Christ.

In August 1997, the Lord allowed me to start seeing a young man who was working with me in the Youth Ministry at First Baptist Church of Glenarden. We had been working together as youth advisors. Both of us had an interest in helping young people. We met in this ministry, and the rest is history. We went through premarital counseling for six months and got married in August 1998.

In premarital counseling, we spent six months with a couple who had been married for thirty-seven years. They shared so much with us and taught us how to have a godly marriage. We learned that including Jesus Christ and practicing the principles of God's word would be the best route for us to take. We both wanted a marriage that would make God proud. We made a decision that we were going to live by the principles of God in our marriage.

If anyone were to ask me the key to a successful marriage, I would say having an active relationship with Jesus Christ. God created the institution called marriage. Therefore, when we decide to live by His word, and obey His principles, we can't go wrong. This doesn't mean that the marriage is perfect, but it means that you will always have someone who is bigger than you or your mate who is fighting for your relationship to work. God is the key! However, He is a gentleman and must be invited into your marriage. He doesn't force himself on anyone. Once you invite Him in, He will be there to make the marriage more than you ever could imagine.

There have been times where I would have said or did the wrong thing, but because of my relationship with Jesus Christ, I said the right thing (or didn't say anything at all). Jesus has kept me sweet at times when I know that I could have been mean. He has kept me married when times were tough and I thought of running away. He has given me peace when the cares of this world have had me so troubled. Jesus Christ has made all of the difference in my marriage. There is no way that we would still be married without the Lord. He is a keeper! He can keep your marriage like no one else can. If you don't know Him and haven't invited Him into your life, I encourage you to let Him in.

Your life and your marriage will never be the same. He can make a bad marriage good and good marriage even greater. Jesus is the glue that will hold a marriage together. Try Jesus!

JOINT ACCOUNTS

Why is it that couples will quickly join everything together except their bank accounts? I have found that couples will quickly kiss and join their saliva; be intimate and join their bodily fluids; share homes, cars, food, and everything, but when it comes to the money, there is some hesitation. Sometimes, couples will come together in many of these areas before marriage, but refuse to have a joint account. We should not join together in holy matrimony if we are not willing to join our money.

God designed marriage for two people to come together as one entity. In Genesis 2:24, it says that two shall become one flesh. This means that a husband and wife should function as one. I do understand the hesitation. When you work hard to earn the money, you certainly don't like the idea of someone else having free access to spend it. However, we must trust God and bring our resources together.

Oneness in finances is a challenge, but it is one worth taking. It is definitely a God idea. Therefore, He will help you and your mate to manage a joint account. I remember when we first got married. We went to the bank and opened up our joint account. We made so many mistakes in the beginning. I was taking money out without communicating with William, and he was doing the same thing. A few times, we had checks that bounced because we were not communicating about our daily financial transactions. After numerous mistakes were made, we came together and laid down some ground rules to make the joint account work. We decided that we must talk about our spending habits. We had to let each other know when we had written checks on the account and when we made a withdrawal. Communication is the key to successfully managing a joint account.

One of the benefits of following this principle is that it creates oneness. There really should not be any statements like "This is my money" and "That is your money." When you are one, everything is ours. The more areas in your marriage that are separated, the easier it is to separate. We need to be tied, bonded, and working together. When your bank accounts are together, it strengthens your relationship. Trust God and try it!

JOY

Do you have joy in your marriage? Have you found joy in your mate? Joy is a necessary emotion that God wants us to experience in our mate and our marriage relationship. However, we can only experience true joy through Jesus. I purposely chose the word *joy* and not happiness, because happiness is based on what happens. And sometimes we will have some things that happen in our marriage that don't make us happy. Joy is an emotion that is eternal. In John 12:11, Jesus says, "These things I have spoken to you, that my joy may remain in you, and that your joy may be full." Joy is based on our relationship with the Lord. When we have the Lord living in our hearts, we can always have joy. We don't have to worry about it running out. The scripture says that the joy of the Lord shall be our strength (Nehemiah 8:10). We need God's joy so that we can experience true joy in our mates and our marriage. He will teach us how to find pleasure in our mates. We can experience an abundance of joy in our mates and our marriage when we have Jesus living and abiding in our heart. When was the last time that you let your spouse know that it is a joy just to be with them?

CHAPTER ELEVEN
THE *K* PRINCIPLES

KEEPING IT TOGETHER

My grandmother taught me that the same things that I did to attract my husband are the same things that I need to do to keep my husband's attraction. When we were courting, I was so careful about how I looked; my hair, dress, and shoes had to be right. I spent extra time in the mirror, getting myself together. I learned that men are attracted by what they see. Therefore, I want to make sure that I am presenting myself to my husband in an attractive way.

As the years progress, our bodies change and we age. However, I believe that we should work very hard at maintaining our appearance. Some people go out of their way to win their mate's attraction during the beginning of the relationship, but after they have been together for some time, they act like they just don't care. In 1 Peter 3:3 it says, "Do not let your adornment be merely outward arranging the hair, wearing gold, or putting on fine apparel but let it be the hidden person of the heart." This verse lets us know that there should be some adornment on the outside. However, there should be more emphasis on the inner beauty.

I do believe that beauty starts on the inside. This is one of the reasons why I start the day with prayer, reading God's word, and spending time with the Lord. I know that it is He who makes me beautiful from the inside out. I want to keep myself presentable for me and for my husband. I want him to always be proud to introduce me to his friends.

The principle of keeping yourself together is all about being beautiful from the inside out, Maintaining your hair, body, clothes, and the way that your present yourself on a daily basis. Maintenance takes time and money. It takes time to do your hair (or to have someone else do it). It takes time to exercise and to select nutritional meals to eat. It also takes time to shop and keep your clothes maintained. The goal is to keep yourself presentable and attractive to yourself and to your mate. I love to see couples who have been married for twenty-plus years, and you can see that they both believe in this principle. We only have one body, and it is up to us to maintain our bodies in such a way that honors God. Exercising self-control is crucial. If we let ourselves go, we may find ourselves eating everything, and this will show in our body.

As a wife, you need to find out what turns your husband on. Some men have a particular thing that they are attracted to. My husband is very particular about my hair. He insists on me having it freshly washed and styled every week. One of my girlfriends said that her husband's preference is her feet. He loves to see her feet with a fresh pedicure. If your husband has an area that he is particular about, as a wife, you need to know what that area is and aim to please. This principle goes both ways. A husband needs to follow the same principle. Keep yourself together!

KINDNESS

I find it so interesting that in 1 Corinthians 13:4, the word of God says that love suffers long and is kind. *Kindness* and *suffering* are two words that don't normally go together. When I am suffering, I am not thinking about being kind, especially to the person who is making me suffer. Let's face it, when you are married for any length of time, there will be some suffering. According to this verse, the suffering may be for a long time. Sometimes, it seems so unfair, because when you become one with a person, you may have to suffer because of something that he or she has said or done. The suffering may not have had anything to do with your actions, but because the two become one, you have to suffer with your mate.

Whatever the reason for the suffering, God has commissioned us to suffer and still be kind to each other. This doesn't make any human sense. When someone is causing you to suffer or when you are experiencing something in your marriage that is causing you to suffer, being kind is usually not your first approach. It is only through the power of Jesus Christ that I can be kind in the midst of suffering.

Kindness is expressed by the way we talk to each other, the way that we treat each other, and the way that we behave. God is asking us to be gentle, tender, and compassionate, and to have a willingness to be good to our mates in the midst of suffering. The only way that I have been able to apply this principle is by having an intimate relationship with

Jesus Christ. The more time that I spend getting closer to God through praying and reading His word, He transforms the way that I act and the way that I think. When my mind and my thoughts are covered with the word of God and the ways of God, I can be kind in the midst of suffering. Jesus Christ suffered, bled, and died on the cross, and never once did He cuss and fuss. When Jesus lives within you, He gives you the same power.

Jesus gives us power to love and be kind even though our flesh wants to rise up and be mean and angry. The more time that I spend with the Lord, the more He teaches me how to be kind toward my husband. He will place things on my heart to say and to do that I know could only come from Him. He has given me kindness to give to my husband in the midst of some stormy situations. This is really when my husband is able to see Christ in me. Anyone can be kind when everything is going well, but it takes a true relationship with Jesus Christ to help you to be kind in the midst of a suffering situation. Have you been kind to your mate?

KING

When I think of a king, I think of royalty. I think of a man sitting in a beautiful chair trimmed in gold. I can imagine lots of servants around him, ready to move at his command. I think of a man who receives great honor and respect, and the people look up to him. One of the sayings that I frequently heard when I got married is, "Treat your husband like a king." They say if you treat him like a king, he will treat you like a queen. I am not sure if every woman would agree with the last part, because I have heard women say, "I treat him like a king, but he doesn't know how to treat me."

I have found that my relationship with the King of Kings (Jesus Christ) has taught me how to treat my earthly king (William Tatem). I have learned to honor him, respect him, and serve him. When you think of your husband as your king, you take on a royal mentality. Your desire should be to please the king. You can please the king in your actions, your talk, the way that you dress, and how you serve him. Queen Esther spent twelve months preparing herself to go into the presence of the king. How do you prepare yourself before going into your husband's presence?

Whenever you are not in agreement with your king, or you feel that he is not in line with the King of Kings, you must pray. The Bible says that the king's heart is in the hand of the Lord, and He directs it like a watercourse wherever He pleases (Proverbs 21:1). Just know that God is able to change and direct your husband's heart. As a wife, you have to learn to use spiritual tools, such as prayer and godly conduct, to make an impact on your king (1 Peter 3:1).

Treating your husband like a king is all about loving, honoring, serving, and presenting yourself in such a way that pleases him. God is pleased when His daughter treats His son like a king!

KISSING

How often do you affectionately kiss your mate? Something as simple as joining your lips with your husband or wife on a daily basis can be a way that we express our affection and our love. Affectionate kissing can help to start a fire that will burn all day until you are able to add more wood. Why is it that affectionate kissing is often seen in the movies but as time goes on, husbands and wives seem to leave this out of their daily lives?

We often give the routine kiss, which is a kiss to say good-bye or a kiss to say hello, but the passionate tongue kiss is often a thing of the past in some marriage relationships.

Oftentimes, it was a kiss that initiated our affection and passion for our mate, but as time goes on, we reduce to a peck on the lips. Are the long and passionate kisses only for the movies? No. It is an expression of affection that can help to stimulate other forms of affection.

Studies have shown there are so many benefits to kissing. It has been said that men and women who start their day with a passionate kiss have a better day. Kissing brings couples closer together, it is a form of bonding, and it is a great practice that can be applied to help your marriage stay strong and help you to live long. Studies state that a kiss is not just a kiss. It feels good and it is good for you. In an article by Ae Dechavez it states that "Lovers who frequently make out are proven to be more satisfied and committed to their relationship." The passionate kiss stimulates juices in the brain that are healthy. Never underestimate the power of a passionate kiss (just make sure that your breath is fresh so that the kiss will be pleasant). Why not make it a practice to passionately kiss each day?

CHAPTER TWELVE
THE *L* PRINCIPLES

LEAVE AND CLEAVE

In marriage, a man is instructed to leave his father and his mother and be joined to his wife (Genesis 2:24). This means that once a man marries, he should leave his parents' household and establish his own household with his wife. God intends for the husband and wife to be joined together as one. I think that it is interesting that a man is instructed to leave his mother and his father. This does not mean that he is not to see them again; it just means that God is making it clear that a husband and wife must establish their own territory and not play house in Mom and Dad's home. The man is being instructed to be joined or to cleave to his wife. He is to hold onto her, embrace her, and bond with her without there being others to hinder the bonding process.

When a man does not leave his mother and father's house, it is hard for him to cleave. This really creates a problem. Some men are Mama's boys, and they really don't want to leave Mama. When the wife has to move in with her husband and his mama, it makes it very difficult for the bonding to take place. This is why the Lord says leave and cleave. We must remember that the creator of marriage knows the best principles on making a marriage work. When we follow God's principles on marriage, we will experience success. Leave and cleave!

LINGERIE

What are you wearing to bed? Is your spouse pleased with what you wear to bed? Have you asked him or her? Wearing what is cozy, comfortable, and warm is not always pleasing to your spouse. Wives, remember that husbands are often attracted by what they see. They like what looks good to the eye and feels good to the touch. Usually, it doesn't take much; in fact, less is better. My husband calls it "putting on something small." What you wear to bed often affects what goes on in the bed. Therefore, you need to be selective about what you wear to bed. Most of us know how to make ourselves look pretty when we are going to work or outside of the home. However, looking good in bed is just as important.

I have heard so many men say, "I wish that she would get rid of those flannel pajamas." I love lingerie. At the beginning of our marriage, I vowed to wear something different to bed every night. It has been over eleven years, and I am still wearing something small and different every night. I have found that wearing something different to bed every night has created a level of excitement in our bedroom. My husband will often come in and take a peak under the covers just to see what I am wearing. My lingerie will often set the mood.

I have heard some women say that their husbands are cool with them wearing a T-shirt to bed, and this may be true. So find out what kind of lingerie or bed attire turns your husband on and wear it. It may not even take any of that. Oftentimes, the lingerie is only on for a few minutes, and then it has served its purpose. Ask your husband about his preference, and wear whatever turns him on. Don't be afraid to try different styles of lingerie. Take a look at your bed attire. Is it pleasing and attractive to your husband, or do some changes need to be made?

LOVE

"I love you!" We seem to say these words so quickly and lightly in the beginning of our marriage relationship. Love is an emotion and a decision that is followed by some actions. Most of us feel the emotions, and we can quickly say "I love you" in the beginning because the relationship is new and perhaps you haven't experienced anything that would make you not want to love your mate. It's very easy to love when things are going the way that you would like, you are being treated the way that you like, and there is money in the bank. However, there are times in marriage where the love doesn't flow easily. This is why a relationship with God is so important. God is love, and when we have a relationship with Him, we can go to love and get love to give to your spouse. When you feel like you don't have anything else in you to give, you can go to God and get what you need to sustain your marriage relationship. The Bible says that love never fails. God's love never fails. We don't have this type of love in and of ourselves. We need the love of God in our marriage.

Some marriages have gotten to the point where they ask, "Where is the love?" I have heard a wife say that her husband doesn't love her anymore. Well, in and of ourselves, our love tank can dry up. However, when we get connected with the Giver of Love, we don't have to run out. Jesus will keep the love of God flowing in our hearts. Remember, it is His desire that we are married from death do us part. So, God wants to keep supplying us with everything that we need to stay in love with our husband or wife. God is there, waiting on us to come to Him. He will give us a fresh supply every day.

One of the lessons that God taught me about love is to love my husband regardless of the circumstances. It is a decision to continue to treat him with love and respect, no matter what we are going through. In 1 Corinthians Chapter13, the Bible teaches us the attributes of love. I would recommend that every husband and wife read it and strive to put it into practice. It teaches us the way that God designed for us to love. However, we must have God in our hearts to love the way that He teaches us to love.

CHAPTER THIRTEEN
THE *M* PRINCIPLES

MANAGE

As a wife and a mother, there is so much that I must manage in order to keep our house and family in good standing. With the exception of a few things, I normally manage the inside of our home. William manages everything on the outside, such as mowing the lawn, washing the cars, and emptying the trash. He also is the one who does the grocery shopping and quite a bit of the cooking. The ability to manage is very important. I have found that managing is a little more challenging when you are working outside of the home. During the time that I was a stay-at-home mom, I felt that I was better able to manage the things in the home. Now that I am working, it requires more discipline and commitment to get my work done. Managing is a job that requires work and skills in several areas.

First, I manage our home: Making sure that it is kept clean and well stocked with all of the supplies that are needed and teaching the children how to help with the chores. I also manage everyone's closet. As the seasons change, I make sure that everyone has the clothes that he or she needs for the season. Since my children are constantly growing, I check to see what they can fit and what we need to give away. Although everyone pitches in, I oversee the overall management of the home.

Second, I manage our family schedule. I keep track of every appointment, celebration, and activity that each of us are involved in. Usually, I mark the calendar and make sure that everyone gets to their destination in a timely fashion. This also includes the kids' homework and special projects. Since my kids are young, I make sure that their important dates are noted and that their work is turned in on time.

Third, I manage our family finances. This includes maintaining a budget, saving, paying bills, and seeing to it that everyone has the things that he or she needs.

Every household is different. However, every home needs to be managed. Most of the time, whichever person is better at managing is the one who does the job.

MANNERS

As a child, I can remember being told to always use my manners: Say please, thank you, no thank you, and excuse me when necessary. As I got older and started learning more about hospitality, I learned to ask my guests "Would you like something to drink?" or "Can I get you something?" I also learned the principle of doing everything that I could to make my guests feel special when they enter my home.

While being married, I have learned that the same principles that apply to my guests should apply to my husband. I must admit he is better at using his manners toward me than I am toward him. I think this is because he is a southern man. He learned to use his manners well, and I have learned from him. For the past eleven years, he has always opened doors for me. He opens the car door and any other door. When he goes out and he knows that I am home, he calls and asks, "Can I bring you anything?" If we are out and we are on our way home, he will ask, "Would you like to stop and get anything before we go home?" When I am at home and he is fixing something to eat, he will ask me, "Would you like something?" It was early in our marriage that he taught me the principle of asking guests, "Would you like something to drink?" or "Can I get you something?" after a few minutes of a guest being in our home.

Guests should be treated special, and so should your spouse. Some people will bend over backwards for a guest who enters their home but treat their spouse like an enemy. It really doesn't make any sense to give a guest the royal treatment when your spouse is starving for the royal treatment from you. So the point that I am making here is to use your manners with your spouse. When you are home, take a moment from what you are doing and ask, "Can I get you something to drink? Would you like anything? How may I serve you?" Our mate should not have to go to someone else or someone else's house to get the royal treatment. We should be able to count on the royal treatment from the king or the queen that God has blessed us to marry.

I believe that the closer I get to God, the more He teaches me how to serve, love, and treat my husband right. In 1 Corinthians 13:4–5 it says that love is kind, and that it does not behave rudely. When we do not use our manners, we are being rude. *Manners* can be defined as the way that we behave with reference to polite standards. To be rude is to be discourteous or impolite. It can also mean to be rough, harsh, or ungentle. The Lord has commissioned us to be kind and to use our manners. Ladies, when was the last time that you asked your husband, "Can I get you something to drink?" Husbands, when was the last time that you opened the door for your wife? Use your manners!

MIRROR

What does your marriage look like? If you were to put your marriage in front of a mirror, what reflection would you see? Genesis 1:27 says, "So God created man in His own image, in the image of God He created him; male and female He created them." Therefore, our marriage should reflect Christ and the relationship that He had with the church. Christ loved the church so much that He gave his life for the church. He suffered, bled, and died for the church. When people see your marriage, they should see love, and it should be a reflection of the love that Christ had for the church. We should make marriage look so attractive that everyone wants what we have. I heard people say that when they see President Obama, Michelle Obama, and their children, it makes them want to be married with children.

Our marriage should demonstrate the love of Christ. Since we are created in the image of Christ, people should be able to look at us and see God. This means that we should love and serve each other, be kind to each other, and be genuinely happy to be together. Keeping our marriage commitment regardless of the obstacles that may come up is one way to reflect Christ. Are people able to experience the love of Christ when they are in the presence of your marriage? Wherever you go, your marriage should be a reflection of Christ. People should be able to see something different when they see your marriage. The love of Christ and a love for each other will make a marriage shine. So make sure that your marriage mirrors Christ.

MULTIPLY

I remember the word *multiply* being used in two ways during our marriage counseling. I was told that oftentimes, a woman will multiply whatever a man dishes out. So if he treats her like dirt, she will multiply this feeling. Likewise, if he loves, honors, and cherishes her, she will multiply the same treatment toward her husband. This statement may not be true for all, but I have found that some women operate this way. I say "some," because depending upon your relationship with the Lord, you may choose not to multiply anything that is not good. So if your husband is acting like a fool, you may decide that you are still going to treat him with love.

The other thing that I was told was to "be fruitful and multiply" (Genesis 1:22). This usage of the word *multiply* refers to having children. Back in the ancient times, having lots of children was a symbol of blessings and strength. Today, some couples get married without a desire or plan to have any children. However, one of the purposes of marriage is to have children and raise a godly seed. Imagine what the world would be like if we didn't multiply. God intended for us to be fruitful and multiply. He wants us to raise children who will bring glory and honor to Him. Children are rewards that can only be given from the Lord. The Bible says, "Happy is the man who has his quiver full of children" (Psalm 127:5).

CHAPTER FOURTEEN
THE *N* PRINCIPLES

NAGGING

One principle that I learned early in my marriage is that men don't like naggers. My husband had a big problem with me asking him to do something and then, when he didn't do it, I would come back to him again and again until it was done. Another form of nagging is constantly complaining or making a demand for your spouse to do something. I quickly learned that there is a way to get my husband to respond and to move, but nagging was not the way.

There are two verses in scripture that have helped me to understand the negative effect that nagging has on a man. The first verse is Proverbs 21:9: It is better to live on a corner of a roof than to share a house with a nagging wife. This verse tells me that a man would rather be on top of a roof in a corner than to come home to a wife who is nagging him. The second verse is Proverbs 21:19: It is better to live in a desert than to live with a nagging, angry wife. Now, this verse says that it is better for a man to live in a hot, dry land where there is no water than to live in a house with a nagging and angry wife. Reading these verses emphasizes the need for a wife to control her tongue. One friend of mine told me that he has driven home from work and parked away from his house just to sit in the car before entering his home. He had to prepare himself to be able to walk into his home. His wife was a nagger, and he had to prepare himself to deal with her mouth before he walked in the house. After a while, he didn't want to come home at all because the thought of his nagger was running him away. The Bible says that death and life are in the power of the tongue; imagine how many women are killing their husbands with their tongue. When a man is killed by his wife's tongue, it is hard for her to bring him back to life. She has to pray and ask God to help her to use her tongue in the proper way to rebuild her husband. Learning when to speak and when not to speak and how to speak are valuable lessons. In 1 Peter 3:4 it states that a wife with a gentle and quiet spirit is very precious in the sight of the Lord.

NEGATIVE

One of my friends said that she has been married for twenty-something years and has always had problems with her mother-in-law mistreating her. So one day, her husband had to take a stand and tell his mother that he was not going to tolerate her mistreating his wife any longer. Although my friend had discussed this with her husband many times, it took a long time for her husband to stand up to his mom. There are some mothers who do not respect their son's choice in marriage; therefore, they make it hard for their daughter-in-law. It's a terrible thought but the reality is that everyone is not for your marriage. The negative principle is all about handling any relationships or anything that threatens or weakens your marriage in any way. There will be some people who have a negative impact on you, your spouse, or your marriage. If you find that a person doesn't have anything good to say about your spouse, this is a problem. Your family, friends, and associates may not be happy about your choice of a mate. Therefore, they may create a negative environment when you bring your spouse around.

Anyone who is not for your marriage is against it. If there is someone who makes you or your spouse feel threatened, it needs to be addressed. Once it is addressed, time should be given for the problem to be corrected. If it is not corrected, then you may have to take other actions to get rid of the negative relationship.

If you go out and spend time with a "friend" who says things that make you feel or think negatively about your husband, you need to examine this friendship. When a "friend" or family member makes your spouse feel threatened, you should first reassure your mate and then address the issue and take a stand for your spouse. I use quotes for "friend" because a true friend would accept you and your mate. Since the two become one, when friends love and accept you, they should do the same for the mate of your choice. When family members cannot accept the person who you have made a covenant with, you will have to separate yourself. Your relationship with your spouse should be the most important human relationship that you have. No one or nothing should be allowed to threaten or weaken your marriage relationship.

NOTICE

Have you ever experienced getting a new hair cut, color, or style, and no one seems to have noticed? Well, this principle is all about being aware of the little things that may change from day to day. It is often the things that we noticed in the beginning of our relationships that made us attractive to each other (the outward appearance, the smile, laugh, voice, etc.). I have found that women and men have a need to be noticed. I have made it a practice to notice when my husband gets his hair cut and to compliment him on how nice he looks. Sometimes, we take each other for granted, and life can become so routine that we don't take time to notice and give compliments when compliments are due. I love receiving a compliment from my husband. When I make a change in my physical appearance (change my hair, eyebrows or shed a few pounds), I want my husband to notice and to make a positive comment. We all need to be told how nice we look, or how nice our haircut looks. I don't want my husband or my children to be starving for compliments.

When a man goes out of his way to do something that he normally would not do, he wants his wife to notice. Let's say he doesn't normally help with housework. However, you express a desire for your husband to do more. One day, he decides to clean the house and help with the children. If you come home and never say one word about the change that you see, it may be a long time before he does it again.

When we don't take the time to notice, we often miss the opportunity to give compliments when compliments are due. Therefore, we open the door for someone else to come along and feed this need. We should study our mates so well that we notice changes and improvements that they make from day to day. After you notice, give a compliment.

NOURISH

I was talking to a newlywed the other day, and she was having a difficult time because she felt like her husband didn't care about her. He tells her that he loves her, and I really believe that he loves her. However, she wants him to show that he cares. The examples that she shared were 1) "If I come home from work at five o'clock every day, and one day I am late, I would like for him to call me to say, 'Are you okay?' I want him to check on me throughout the day." 2) "If I am hurt, I want him to naturally come and check on me." 3) She expressed that she wanted him to give her the time, care, and attention that he may give to his job, computer, and church work.

As I listened to this young lady's concerns, I couldn't help but think of the word *nourish*. She wants her husband to do a better job of nourishing. To nourish is to support, sustain with food or nutriment, to protect and to supply what is necessary for life, health and growth. However, if there was no one to properly nourish you as a child it will be difficult for you to know how to nourish others as an adult. Sometimes, we don't get things from our spouse because he or she doesn't know how to give them.

Ephesians 5:28-29 says that a husband ought to love his wife as his own body. It also states that "He who loves his wife loves himself." This passage explains that just as the Lord nourishes and cherishes the church, a husband is to nourish and cherish his wife. So for those who may not have been properly nourished as a child, God is able to teach you. Since it is His desire that a husband nourishes and cherishes his wife, all you have to do is ask God to teach you how to nourish. As we go to Him, we must ask God to show us how to specifically love, cherish and nourish our mate. I believe that whatever we lack due to our environment and the way that we were raised, God wants to meet the need. Remember that God knows us and our mate better than we know ourselves. Therefore, if we ask Him, He will teach us. In addition to asking God, we should ask our mates, "How would you like for me to nourish you?" We have to teach each other how we would like to be loved. Once a husband or a wife has communicated how he or she would like to be nourished, as a mate, we should aim to please. Nourish and cherish your mate!

CHAPTER FIFTEEN
THE *O* PRINCIPLES

OBEDIENCE

As I think about everything that has been created, I notice that they come with a set of instructions or rules. For example, as children, we had parents or guardians who provided us with rules as to how we should live. In school, we had teachers and administrators who gave us instructions on how to do our work. On a job, we have a boss or owner who gives us instructions on how our work should be done. When the instructions or rules are followed, there are rewards. Every electronic device that we use comes with a set of instructions from the manufacturer that tells us how to use the device. Whenever we read the rules and follow the instructions, there is an expected outcome. In many cases, the parent, teacher, boss, or manufacturer already knows the outcome. Their job is to get people to follow the rules or instructions and do the work so that the best results will come.

One word that sums up all of this is *obedience*. Obedience is being willing to obey, to follow the instructions, the commands, or the wishes of someone else. Well, when God created marriage, he created it with some wishes, commands, and instructions. In order for us to get the best results, we have to follow the wishes of the manufacturer. God's instructions for marriage are written in His word: the Bible. When a husband and wife decide to include the principles of God in their marriage and obey what the word says, they position themselves to be blessed.

Psalm 119:1 says, "Blessed are those who walk in the law of the Lord." In Joshua 1:8, the Lord told Joshua, "This Book of the Law shall not depart from your mouth, but you shall meditate in it day and night, that you may observe to do according to all that is written in it. For then, you will make your way prosperous, and then you will have good success." This prosperity and success means much more than financial success. It includes spiritual and marital well-being. Obedience to the Lord is the key to true success.

ON TIME

Do you know of couples who are always late? Every time you invite them somewhere, you can count on them showing up late. Well, this principle is very simple. Most couples will receive many invitations in the course of their married years. Often, the invitation requires you to attend as a couple. Strive to be a couple who shows up on time. Don't be known as the couple who is always late. Showing up on time says a lot about you, and showing up late to every event says something about you as well. Which do you want to be remembered for?

Whenever you are invited somewhere, allow yourself enough time so that you can show up when expected. Someone needs to gather all of the necessary information ahead of time. This information could consist of the address, the time, the actual invitation, and directions to wherever you need to go. If you don't have all of your information gathered in advance, this could cause you to run late or miss the event altogether. You can miss a lot of important things if you have a habit of being late. Sometimes, it is hard to break this habit. You can become comfortable with showing up late. Arrive on time and experience events from the beginning to the end.

OPEN

The open principle refers to being naked and not ashamed with each other. A husband and wife should be able to share their innermost thoughts and their bodies with each other. This principle also refers to being open to what God wants to do in your marriage.

"And they were both naked, the man and his wife, and were not ashamed" (Genesis 2:25). Adam and Eve were physically naked; however, I believe that this verse means that they were comfortable with each other. Being naked means they were comfortable in their physical bodies, in their sexuality, in their relationship, and in their work. Imagine if we are comfortable enough to be open in all of these areas. When a husband and wife can be totally open about how they feel, there is freedom.

There have been situations in our marriage that I have talked about and didn't feel like I was being heard; therefore, I stopped talking.

When I stopped talking about the issue, I began to unconsciously hold back in other areas. Concealment creates a wall. Now I honestly feel like I can talk to William about everything. I didn't always feel this way; over time our relationship has grown stronger, and I now feel comfortable enough to be open about everything. Although some topics are more delicate than others, I still feel that I can be open about how I feel. Being able to share my innermost feelings with my husband is therapeutic and freeing. He doesn't always understand or agree with the way that I feel, but I find so much pleasure in releasing my thoughts. When we are open with each other, we are able to learn more about each other. We learn what makes each other tick, we learn how to better love each other, and we learn how to be sensitive to each other's needs. Concealing who we are is like hiding a part of yourself from the person God intended for you to be one with. The oneness is hard to achieve when you can't share your innermost self with the one you have vowed to spend the rest of your life with.

The other part of this principle is simply being open to what God is going to do in your marriage. We never know some of the things that God has in store for us. Therefore, we need to be open. It may be doing something that you have never done before, like adopting a child, going on a mission trip, feeding families in need, leaving your job and becoming a homemaker, and so on. Pray and seek God so that you can hear what God has designed for your marriage.

The open principle is all about being yourself and sharing your innermost thoughts with your mate. Also, being open to what God wants to do in and through your marriage.

OPEN DOORS

When I first started dating William, he opened the car door for me, and if we were entering a store or any building, he would open the door. I was not used to this treatment, and it took me a while to accept and embrace his desire to serve me in this way. My original thought was, "I can open my own doors," and it was quicker for me to just get out of the car on my own. However, he insisted on serving me in this way. It bothered him when I would get out of the car on my own or when I would walk into a building and not allow him to get the door for me.

I must admit, having my husband to always be mindful of me when he gets out of a car and when we are going into a building really makes me feel special. This is often a practice of the past because some women insist on opening their own doors (and some men have not been taught the value of serving a lady in this way). When we were dating, I wondered how long this would last. However, it's been over eleven years, and he is still opening the car doors and the doors of any building that we enter together. So ladies, when your husband wants to open doors for you, embrace it! We have to learn to receive the blessings that God wants to give us through our mates. We can encourage our husbands in this area by sitting in the car until he comes around to open the door and by standing to the side to allow him to open the door as we enter a building.

CHAPTER SIXTEEN
THE *P* PRINCIPLES

PARENTS

Your parents can help to make your marriage relationship or help to break it. One of the things that I learned in premarital counseling was to be careful about the things that I shared with my parents about my marriage and my husband. My stepfather passed away before I got married, so the closest parents to me are my mom and grandparents. You see, I know that my parents love me, and they love William. However, I was taught that there would be some difficult times in marriage, and it is very important that I don't paint an ugly picture of my marriage or William when times get rough. If I shared every argument or disagreement with my mom, she might have a negative view of my husband. Sharing negative comments about William with my mom might cause her not to like William or to have something against him. Later, I may forget about the argument and forgive William. However, my mom may never be able to get over the comments that I shared.

Most parents love their children dearly, and you should not put them in situations where they are forced to take sides with you. I vowed to never put my husband down or share any of his flaws with my parents. All they hear are the positives. I pray about the negatives and the things that I would like to see changed.

Another valuable lesson that I have learned is not to rely on your parents for things that your spouse should provide. For example, John and Janet get married. Janet has been used to calling on her dad to come to her rescue whenever she has car trouble. After she gets married, she doesn't learn to switch her needs to her husband, so she still expects her dad to come to her rescue. Her car breaks down and she calls on her dad first. Dad comes and pays for the car to be towed and repaired. His thought may be, "Anything for my daughter."

This may not sound like a problem, but once this happens over and over, throughout years of marriage, this will create a problem. John may feel that Janet does not need him and that her father is always going to come to her rescue. He hasn't had a chance to come to his wife's rescue because she immediately invites her father in instead of her husband. Over time, this creates a wedge between John and his father-in-law. John doesn't know how to tell his father-in-law to allow him the opportunity to come to his wife's aid. The father-in-law could help in this matter by teaching Janet to go to her husband.

When you are married, you have to learn to allow your spouse the opportunity to come to your rescue. Although parents are often dependable and financially prepared to help, you have got to learn to stop relying on them. When unexpected situations occur, your spouse should be given the opportunity to come to the rescue. Don't rely on your parents for things that you and your spouse should supply to each other.

PHONE CALLS

I know that we live in a generation where sending a text message is popular, but have you ever thought about the power of a phone call? The phone is a great tool that can be used to build great communication in a marriage. Although I like to send my husband a text message every now and then, I believe that communicating on the phone offers something that I can't get from a text message. I can't hear my husband's voice when I send a text message. Hearing his voice helps me to discern a lot about what is going on with him. When my husband began working two jobs, he started being away from home for several hours. However, due to the telephone, I have never felt like he is gone for as long as he actually is gone. During the day when both of us are at work, we connect at least two times, at lunch and at the end of our work day. I will call him, or he will call me. Our conversations are always brief. We ask how each other's day is going, and we discuss our plans for the kids, dinner, or anything that is taking place on that day. Therefore, when we see each other at the end of the day, we have an idea of the kind of day that we both have had. Sometimes, our days are good, and sometimes, something has happened to challenge our day. However, we talk about it, and it makes us sensitive to each other's feelings and mood for later that evening.

Using the phone to stay in touch throughout the day helps to build a closeness between you and your mate. There have been times where I have misplaced my cell phone or left home without it, and I could not connect with my husband during the day. Neither one of us liked the feeling of going all day without connecting. Using the phone to connect when you are away is a great way to keep the lines of communication open. I think we take so much for granted from day to day. We assume that we will leave home, go to work, and come back home every day. However, we really don't know if we will make it home every evening. Anything could happen in the course of a day. I would not want to assume that all is well and not call my husband during the day. I would rather talk to him and know that all is well. Therefore, if anything were to happen, I would have connected with him.

Today, many people love to use their phones to send text messages. This is a powerful tool, because if you can't talk but just want to let your mate know that you are thinking of them, or just to say "I love you," you don't have to call, you can send a text message. A text message with some positive words can do wonders for your marriage: "I appreciate you," "You are a great mother," or "You are a great father" are words that will help to build your mate.

On September 11, 2001, there were many couples who departed for work and never made it home. Some had an opportunity to use their cell phones in the midst of the attacks. The phone call made a big difference. Some were calling to say, "I am okay," and some actually called in the midst of being attacked. However, the phone is a very precious tool that was used to allow couples to connect. There is power in connecting with your mate on a daily basis. Take advantage of the phone and use it to connect and to build up the spouse God has given to you. Never underestimate the power of a call!

PHOTOS

One of the things that I really enjoy is taking pictures. As a single person, I was known for carrying a camera to every event. The only problem was sometimes, I would wait too long to get the pictures developed or I didn't get them developed at all. Over time, I have improved in that area. I frequently take my camera with me, and I am excited about getting them printed right away. Now that I have a digital camera, I get to see the pictures as I take them. I have several memory books that I have created over our eleven years of marriage. I have collected pictures from our honeymoon, my pregnancy, the children as babies, their birthdays, childhood in general, vacations, and so on.

I told William that when I am dead and gone, I want my pictures to speak for me. Just in case the children don't remember some of the things that we have done together, the pictures will serve as a reminder. Lately, I have gone to several funerals at my church. At each of the funerals, I have enjoyed watching the slide show that was created with pictures supplied by family members of the deceased person. The photos speak longer and louder than anyone. Taking pictures is a great way to capture and remember the moments in your marriage relationship. So grab a camera and capture as many moments as you can!

PRAYER

Have you ever hoped that your mate would make a certain decision that you knew was the right choice, but you were not sure if your mate would make the right choice? If you ever experience a situation that is too difficult for you or your mate to handle, try prayer. Prayer is communicating with the Lord. When you talk to your Heavenly Father about a situation, you must trust that God is in control. Nothing can happen unless God gives permission. He is the only one who is able to change a person's heart, plans, or direction, or change any situation. I have found prayer to be the secret to my sanity. Whenever there are situations that overwhelm me, I go to God in prayer. When I go to God and trust Him to work it out, I don't take my frustrations and worries to my husband, because I know that God is the only person who can make a difference.

There have been times when my husband is about to make a decision that I may not totally agree with, and I go to God in prayer and God changes my husband's mind or He changes the situation. Communicating with God about every area of your marriage is a good practice. The Bible says that the effective fervent prayer of the righteous avails much (James 5:16b). God wants us to include Him in our marriage; after all, it's His institution.

We must remember that God knows our mates better than we could ever know them. Therefore, He knows how to orchestrate the events of our lives to create the changes and the effects that we need to have in our lives. There have been things that I wished that my husband would do; I have spoken to him about them and there was still no change.

However, when I learned the power of praying for my husband, I began to take my concerns to the Lord. Prayer changed him in such a way that I could never have imagined. Sometimes, I pray and the prayer is answered quickly. There are some things that I have prayed about in reference to my husband, and it has taken years before the prayer has been answered. What I have found is that sometimes God says yes right away, sometimes He says no, and other times He says wait. Usually, when He says wait, there is something that God wants to do in me while I am waiting. He may want to teach me a lesson while I am believing Him to do something in my husband.

When we pray, God produces results that we could never produce. Therefore, I start every day with prayer. Talking to God before I talk to my husband helps me to present myself in a pleasant way. If it wasn't for me talking to Jesus every morning, I don't think that my husband would really like me. I know that my attitude and my mouth would be different. Communicating with Jesus first thing in the morning makes me sweet and helps me to make wise choices when I am dealing with my husband and my family. Through prayer, God has taught me so many things that I myself would not have thought to do. I believe that when I honor God first thing in the morning, everything else falls into place. Matthew 6:33 says, "But seek ye first the kingdom of God and His righteousness, and all of these things will be added unto you."

I recommend having an individual prayer time and having a time when you and your mate pray together. I have my individual time with God first so that my heart and thoughts are right before I present myself to my husband and family. I really believe that this has been the secret to my success as a wife and a mother. Through prayer, God has shaped and made me over so many times.

Praying with your spouse is powerful! God loves when two come together, agree, and present their request to Him. In the Bible, it says, "When two or three are gathered together in My name, I am there in the midst of them" (Matthew 18:20). Praying together makes a statement to the Lord; it says, "We need you, we can't do this thing called marriage without you, we invite your presence in our marriage." I love to hear my husband pray because it helps me to hear things that are on his heart. It's funny, because he may not tell me directly but he will talk to God about his concerns. When my husband expresses his thoughts to God, I learn about the things that I need to be praying about in my individual time with God.

When we pray, we simply present our thoughts, concerns, and requests, and we take time to thank Him for all that He has already done. Also, we pray for others, such as our children, our family members, our friends, our church, this world, and its leaders. Every day, with all of its issues, cares, and concerns, is worth presenting to the Lord. We never know what a day will bring, and starting the day with prayer helps to prepare you for the day. We must remember that God already knows what is going to happen; therefore, we need to commune with Him so that He can prepare us for the day.

When a husband and wife take time to pray, great things will happen in their marriage. The challenges are not as difficult when you know that you can present them to the Lord of Lords and the King of Kings. While working with couples, I have found that this is an area that the enemy fights. He doesn't want a husband and wife to come together to pray. So, he makes us think that we are too busy, or that our schedules will not permit us to pray. Where there is a will, there is a way. If you can't pray together in person, you can pray over the phone. The important thing is that you come together to talk to the only person who can make a difference in your marriage. Make time to pray with your mate today!

CHAPTER SEVENTEEN
THE *Q* PRINCIPLES

QUARRELS

I can remember a few quarrels that my parents had when I was growing up. I don't remember what the quarrels were about, but I remember the actions of my parents after having the disagreements. Sometimes, they would fuss about something that happened; sometimes, they would fight; and oftentimes, there would be a temporary break in relations. They would both be angry and wouldn't have anything to say to each other for a while. Eventually, they would make up, and everything would be okay. However, I would hate when they argued because I wasn't sure what the final outcome would be.

It is normal to have disagreements in a relationship. However, when we disagree, we must watch our feelings and our actions. Sometimes, we can allow ourselves to get so upset about something that was said or done that really doesn't make any sense. When we become so angry that we are hostile, this will lead to other problems. The Bible is very clear on quarrels. In 2 Timothy 2:23-24 (NIV) it says "Don't have anything to do with foolish and stupid arguments, because you know they produce quarrels. And the Lord's servant must not quarrel, instead he must be kind to everyone, able to teach, not resentful." Only Christ can help us to carry out this scripture.

QUEEN

Imagine what marriage would be like if every husband and every wife had a royal mentality. Husbands would be treated like kings, and wives would be treated like queens. Our service to each other would be five stars, and love would be overflowing. After striving to please God, your desire would be to please your king or your queen. Does this sound too good to be true? Well, I believe that it is possible.

Whenever I dreamed about marriage, I always thought about having a man who would love me and treat me like a queen. From the age of two through my twenties, I was blessed to have a good stepfather in my life. My stepfather passed in 1996. However, because he was my stepfather and I didn't have the love of my biological father, I felt shorted on love from a man. If it wasn't for me giving my life to Christ at the age of twelve, I believe that I would have been looking for love in all the wrong places. My stepfather loved me, but for some reason, I felt like if my biological father loved me, I would have received more hugs, kisses, and affection. So when I began praying for a husband, I specifically asked God to allow him to love the ground that I walked on. Now, I don't know if this sounds right, but to me it meant having a man who really, really loved me, and one who showed his love by treating me like a queen. When God gave me William Tatem, He honored this request.

I believe that my husband could teach a course on how to treat your wife like a queen. William loves me, and he goes out of his way to express his love in so many ways. He is a true servant, so he serves me in some way every day. I love when he opens the doors for me, helps me with the kids, has dinner ready when I get home, helps with cleaning the house and washing the clothes. I don't take these things for granted. I am grateful. He is mindful of me when he makes decisions. He enjoys seeing me look good. He goes out of his way to make sure that I maintain my hair and appearance. He knows how much better I feel when I look good. If I am striving to achieve a goal, he says, "What can I do to help?" and he does things to help me accomplish my goal. He is very supportive in the things that I enjoy doing. I really feel like I am a celebrity and he is my biggest fan! The more that I treat him like a king, the more he treats me like a queen.

QUIET

Did you know that you could win an argument without speaking? Shhhhhsh! One of the most precious things that a woman could have is a quiet spirit. In 1 Peter 3:4 it says that a quiet spirit is very precious in the sight of God. This means that there is great value in learning how to be quiet. Being quiet is truly a skill that comes from the Lord. There are two ways that I have learned to apply this principle.

The first is to do what the word says and just be quiet. Don't say a word. There will be situations or things that happen that you want to respond to with words, but God wants you to bridle your tongue. Sometimes, speaking is more harmful because of what might come out. When a woman learns to be quiet, God begins to speak and move on her behalf. He knows the way that He made us, and being quiet is sometimes the hardest thing to do in marriage. When things are not going our way, or when our husband has made some decisions that we don't agree with, we have some words that "need to be said." So we think the words need to be said. Learn to close your mouth and watch God speak for you. Now when we do this, we have to watch our attitude and conduct. If we are quiet and our actions and attitude are speaking something nasty, then we create a problem. You could be quiet but walk around the house slamming doors and stamping your feet. This is not effective. When we are quiet, we have to learn to give our words to the Lord. He can handle everything that we have to say. As you talk to the Lord, He will shape your attitude and actions to be godly.

The second way that I have learned to apply this principle is to have a quiet spirit. A quiet spirit means exhibiting an attitude that does not demand my personal rights. When I have demanded my personal rights, I might have gotten things my way for the moment, but there was no permanent change in my husband. However, when I exemplify a quiet spirit, I have experienced God working on my husband's heart and creating a permanent change. When God makes a change in my husband, I end up getting what I wanted. I have learned to watch the words that I speak and not to be harsh toward my husband. I am careful in choosing my words because I want to build up and not tear down. So examine your spirit. Are you speaking quietly or loudly? Your voice should be soothing to your husband's ear. Tranquility is the goal. So if you haven't used this principle, ask God to give you a quiet spirit. It does wonders for a marriage.

QUIT

Have you ever had a day where you just felt like quitting? Well, I don't know anyone who has been married for any length of time who can honestly say that the thought has never entered their mind. When there are two imperfect people who come together, striving to live together forever, there will be some problems. Quitting can come to mind because oftentimes in the flesh, it is easier to quit than to persevere. I was taught that a "quitter never wins and a winner never quits." If you want to win in this institution called marriage, you must never quit. When you feel like you want to quit, you must feed yourself with something positive. Seek help from positive friends who are married and want to encourage you to maintain your marriage relationship. Find a positive book that reinforces the principles that help to keep a marriage together. Surround yourself with positive information to encourage you on the marriage journey. I have asked couples who have been married for twenty, thirty, or forty-plus years, "Did you ever feel like quitting?" The answer was, "Yes, but I hung in there, and look where we are today." You can make it, don't quit. It is God's will that you make it in your marriage.

CHAPTER EIGHTEEN
THE *R* PRINCIPLES

RECONCILIATION

Did you know that God specializes in reconciliation? Reconciliation is bringing something together again, causing harmony, restoring something back to its original condition. When a couple gives their marriage to God, He will bring reconciliation. This is a principle that I learned so much about through hearing my pastor preach about marriage. He had shared about not giving up on a marriage because God is able to take a husband and wife who were separated and restore their marriage. It may be years later, but God is able to restore it. There are several couples at our church who have been through major issues, separated, and some divorced, but God brought them back together again. Many of them will testify that when God reconciles their relationship, it is even better than the first time that they were together. God uses His power to help a couple to forgive, heal, and reconnect with their spouse. Since God hates divorce, He loves to reconcile relationships.

This principle became real to me just a few years ago when I witnessed God's reconciliation power on my grandparents. They had been divorced for thirty-five years. My grandmother is seventy-three and my grandfather is seventy-six. Both of them were living in the state of Maryland; however, they had not been together in years. My daughter was in a Christmas program and invited both of her great-grandparents to attend. They both attended and began to reconnect at the Christmas program. Days later, they went out on a date and began talking and dating each other again. The thing that was different this time is that both have a relationship with the Lord and are depending on Him to keep them together. They remarried the next year on Resurrection Sunday because my grandmother said that this is a marriage resurrected by God. Now they are doing wonderfully and enjoying being married. Our entire family has been blessed by their reunion. I am so happy that

God allowed me to personally see and experience His reconciliation power. My grandparents are happier now than they have ever been. I am so glad they have each other for companionship, and neither one of them has to be alone. So don't ever give up on a marriage. Who would have ever thought that after thirty-five years, my grandparents would remarry? God is in the reconciliation business!

RELATIONSHIPS

Building a relationship requires time, love, and commitment. Sometimes, when we are building a marriage, we can get so consumed with each other that we don't make time to build other relationships. If we are not careful, years will go by and we have shut other people out of our lives. Well, I have found that I must be intentional about building other relationships.

The first relationship that I must maintain is my relationship with God. When I spend time in prayer, reading God's word, and being alone with Him, it sets the tone for my day. I am better equipped for everything else when I spend time with the Lord.

The second relationship that I work on is my relationship with my husband. I am mindful of his needs and desires, and make every effort to meet those needs. We make sure that we are communicating throughout the day and that there is harmony. I have to ask myself, have I touched him today? Have I showed him any love today? I realize that it takes daily effort.

The third relationship that I am mindful of every day is my relationship with my children. Have I spent time with them? Have I hugged them and showed them some affection? Did I help with their homework? Have I taken time to hear what is on their heart?

The fourth relationship that I am working on is being mindful of other family members, such as my mom, sister and my grandparents. These are family members I want to be intentional about including in my married life. This means remembering their special dates and making time to spend with them. It may just mean planning to visit on a regular basis. Some family members I see all of the time, and others I have to be more intentional about visiting. However, I realize that life is too short, and if I don't make time to get together, the time will be gone.

The fifth relationship that requires my attention is spending time with friends. I have girlfriends I like to get together with from time to time. Sometimes, a good telephone conversation is all I need. Other times, it is good to be able to meet in person, talk, and have a bite to eat. Most of my friends are married. However, I do have a couple of good friends who are not married, and I try to be mindful of them. Inviting them over from time to time is always fun.

The main point that I want to make here is that although our marriage relationship is the most important human relationship, we still must be mindful of the other people in our lives. We should not get so consumed in our marriage that we are not taking time to build other relationships. Relationships are important, but they require balance. I have heard of some people who are so involved in other relationships that they are not giving their marriage relationship the time and attention that is needed. However, we must have order. God is first; our spouse is next; then our children, family, and friends. If we are not intentional about building these relationships, time will pass us by and we would have never spent time getting to know each other better.

RESPECT

R-E-S-P-E-C-T! Find out what it means to me. I asked my husband what makes him feel respected. His response was 1) being thought of, 2) being included or considered when it comes to making decisions, and 3) coming home to a house that is in order. I was surprised because I thought that his first answer would be, "I feel respected when you speak to me in a nice way or tone." So I asked him about this, and he said, "That too!" But I thought it was interesting that this wasn't the first thing that came out of his mouth. Although every man wants to be respected, there may be different things that make him feel respected. I think it has a lot to do with the type of wife that a man has. For example, some women may not have a problem with the way that they talk to their husband, so he may never feel disrespected by the way that his wife speaks to him. On the other hand, she may have a problem with considering his opinion or thoughts when she makes a decision. Therefore, her husband feels disrespected.

The best way to know how to respect your mate is to ask the question, "What makes you feel respected?" This way, you can make sure that you are meeting the needs of your mate. A husband and wife should respect each other. However, the Bible specifically tells a woman to see to it that she respects her husband (Ephesians 5:33b)."

ROMANCE

"No finance, no romance!" Is this your view? If your money is low, your mate loses his or her job, your bills are not paid, and you can't see your way through, do you deprive your mate? I have heard couples say this. However, if I practiced this, there would be no romance. This is a worldly concept. God never intended for us to mistreat each other or deny each other because of our financial state.

I must say that a woman loves feeling secure. Knowing that the bills are paid and money is coming in makes things easier. However, if these things are not in place, God does not intend for us to be mean and deny each other romance. I have experienced low cash flow and no money coming in. During this time, I had to elevate my mind and separate our financial situation from how I was going to treat my husband in bed. Once I learned to separate our financial situation from our bedroom, we were able to have romance with little or no money. It encouraged my husband to know that I wasn't holding back from him or mistreating him because of our financial state.

After discussing romance with several couples, I have found that women and men see romance differently. Men often define it as doing something special with the intent of having sex. Women define romance as getting flowers, going to dinner, a husband making all of the arrangements to spend time with her, helping her around the house, making a bubble bath for her, and doing special things without necessarily having sex in mind. So I would encourage you to find out how your spouse defines romance and make sure that you take time to practice romance in your marriage.

CHAPTER NINETEEN
THE *S* PRINCIPLES

SEASONS

In every marriage, there are seasons. Have you ever experienced something in your marriage that was so tough, you didn't know if you could stay and endure? Your flesh tells you that you can't take it, and you don't have to take it. Your flesh says you can do better by yourself. Your flesh wonders, how long am I going to have to deal with this? And you really don't see yourself staying in the marriage or making it through the situation. Well, if you continue to feed your flesh with its negative thoughts and desires, then your flesh will win. If you would begin to cast down these thoughts and feed your spirit with thoughts like, "We will make it through this," "I can do all things through Christ, who strengthens me," "I made a covenant to God, and by his power, I will make it," and you ask God to sustain you, keep you, and protect you, You can make it. The flesh constantly fights against the spirit and the things of God. Whichever one you feed the most, will win.

Ecclesiastes 3:1–8 says, "To everything there is a season,
A time for every purpose under heaven;
A time to be born,
And a time to die;
A time to plant,
And a time to pluck what is planted;
A time to kill,
And a time to heal;
A time to break down,
And a time to build up;
A time to weep,
And a time to laugh;
A time to mourn,
And a time to dance;
A time to cast away stones,

And a time to gather stones;
A time to embrace,
And a time to refrain from embracing;
A time to gain;
And a time to lose;
A time to keep,
And a time to throw away;
A time to tear,
And a time to sew;
A time to keep silence,
And a time to speak;
A time to love,
And a time to hate;
A time of war,
And a time of peace."

If we had it our way, there would only be one season, and that would be the good season. This season would only consist of a marriage that is healthy, happy with plenty of love and money. However, if the season was always this way, we would never get to know God as our healer, protector, provider, way maker, and the one who can lift us up. His word lets us know that there will be some changes that we must go through. Oftentimes, marriages don't survive the difficult seasons. Normally, when people decide to leave or when they decide that they can't take it anymore, it is during a difficult season. It is rare that anyone would leave when both are healthy; happy; and getting plenty of love, loving, and money. However, with the help of the Lord, you can weather the storms and make it from one season to the next.

What season are you in right now? When the season changes, you have to change. Just like in nature, when summertime comes, you pull out your lighter garments: shorts, T-shirts, sundresses, sandals, and so on. When winter comes, you pull out your heavier garments: long pants, corduroys, sweaters, coats, and boots. Within our marriage, we have endured some storms, and by the grace of God, we have been able to make it from one season to the next. You can make it through the season by pulling out the garments that are necessary. It might be a garment of long-suffering, kindness, peace, endurance, and strength. All of these things come from having a relationship with God and spending time with Him through prayer, reading His word, and attending a church where your marriage can be strengthened and encouraged. With God, you can make it through any season.

SERVING

"How may I serve you?" This question is like music to my ears when I hear it in a restaurant. Have you ever gone into a restaurant and experienced a waiter who was attentive to all of your needs? He or she stands close by and observes to see when you need something else to drink and when you are ready for something else to eat. Before you have to ask for something, he or she has already predicted your need. Oftentimes, the waiter has been trained to study the customer and to look for certain gestures that indicate a need.

I believe that you should ask the same question in your marriage: How may I serve you? Each of us has certain things that we would like to have our mate do for us. It is not that we can't do these things ourself, but it is more enjoyable when your spouse does it for you. For example, I love having my feet rubbed. Now I can rub my own feet, but it is certainly more enjoyable when William takes the time to rub my feet. As you spend time with your mate, you will notice things that you can help with. There is something that we can do in every room of our house. Think about it! How can I serve my husband in the kitchen? How can I serve my husband in the bedroom? How can I serve my husband in the bathroom? One of the best things to do is to just ask the question: "Honey, how can I serve you? What are some things that you would like for me to do for you?"

When a husband and wife have a servant's heart toward each other, it makes the marriage sweet. Sometimes, we will break our neck to serve everyone but our mate. As a mom, I have found that it's so easy to serve my children and forget about my husband. I had to train myself to consider William. One day, I was washing clothes and God spoke to me. I didn't know if I would finish all of the laundry in one day. Therefore, I wanted to make sure that the kids had everything that they needed washed and folded first. Sometimes, I would get all of their things cleaned but my husband's work uniforms were still waiting to be cleaned. One of the ways that I learned to serve William was making sure that he had a clean uniform and underwear ready for

Monday. Having everything that he needed in the drawer—clean socks, underwear, and a clean uniform—is providing a service. He doesn't ask me to do it, but this is a need that I enjoy taking care of for him.

The best servants are the ones who don't have to be told everything. They have enough experience to predict and know the need before a request is made.

SEX

As a teenager in the church, I was taught to maintain my virginity and that sex is a gift that God gives to married people. At that time, my pastor taught the girls that the most precious thing that you have is your body. Once you give it up to a guy, you have given all that you have. He would encourage the young people to wait until they were married to have sex. He had a number of sayings that were all about maintaining your virginity, and he would say them all the time. He would say, "Anything worth having is worth waiting for. Why buy the cow if you can get the milk free? Keep your dress down and your drawers up. Be a peach out of reach." Hearing these sayings Sunday after Sunday taught me to value and treasure my body. So at the age of twelve, I made up in my mind that my body was precious and that no guy would get my body unless he married me. I didn't want a guy who would come and go; I wanted a husband who would be there to stay.

By the grace of God, I maintained my virginity for twenty-nine years! The Lord helped me to keep my body committed to Him. It was a challenge, especially when I went away to college. God kept me! My husband, William Tatem, was the first. William and I dated for one year before we were married. He knew that I was a virgin and we were both Christians who had decided to be obedient to God by waiting to have sex until after we were married. William had been celibate for over two years before we started dating.

Today, we have a great sex life. I believe that God honored our commitment to wait until we were married so He put a special blessing on our sex life. What makes our sex life great is that I have learned that sex is a need. Some need it more than others. My husband's need is greater than mine. However, I honor the fact that it is a *major* need for him. It's just like having a baby who needs milk. A good mother would never deprive her baby of milk. The baby needs to be fed on a regular basis in order to grow and be healthy and happy. I see my husband's need the same way. When his need is met, he is in a better position to grow, be healthy and happy. I see how having his need met affects him in a positive way.

Since sex is a need, it is a requirement from God for married people. I work really hard to make sure that my husband's need is met. This sometimes means fulfilling the need when I am tired or don't feel like having sex. When I feel this way, I have learned to include God in my bedroom and pray. I ask the Lord to give me what I need so that I can meet my husband's need. God is faithful; He has never let me down. When I pray this prayer, God gives me a burst of energy, and I am able to meet William's need.

I often compare sex to a clear glass of water. If the glass is full and running over, there is no room for more. If the glass is empty, there is room for more water, and if you don't fill the glass, somebody else will. I want to fill my husband's glass so high that it is running over and he never has to think about anybody else filling his glass. Allowing your spouse's glass to be empty for long periods of time opens up the door for temptation. "Do not deprive one another except with consent for a time that you may give yourselves to fasting and prayer, and come together again so that Satan does not tempt you because of your lack of self-control" (1 Corinthians 7:5).

Here are tips that have helped to make our sex life great:
1. Communicate during the day to help set the mood for the night.
2. Bathe, have fresh breath, put on a nice fragrance.
3. Wear nice lingerie. Try wearing something different to bed every night; it helps to stimulate excitement.
4. A husband who helps his wife with household chores and responsibilities helps to ease his wife's mind so that she can be free in the bedroom.
5. Part of sex is mental, so your mind needs to be in it. Prepare your thoughts.
6. Share how you feel with your mate; communicate what turns you on and off.
7. Make sure that your bedroom has the right atmosphere. Remove extra clutter, bills, or anything that takes away from the room being conducive for making love.

8. Know that sexual fulfillment should not be one way. Make sure that both of you have an orgasm.

9. Talk while you are making love. Express your love with words or just make a sound.

10. Make love as often as you can! After all, sex was created for marriage.

SUBMISSION

During our wedding ceremony, Pastor John K. Jenkins, Sr. took a moment to explain the big "S" word. I can remember him saying that it is easy to say that you will submit until you have been asked to do something that you really don't want to do. Most of us have heard the scripture that says, wives, be submissive to your own husbands (Ephesians 5:22). Some husbands will beat this scripture over your head. However, I love the fact that there is also a scripture that says, submit one to another (Ephesians 5:21). After eleven years of marriage, I can think of several occasions where submission was required on both parts. However, I can see why women can have issues with submitting. It's very hard to submit when you feel that you are right and what you are saying makes the most sense. Submission requires you to put your view to the side and go along with your husband. He may not be right, but perhaps God wants to teach him a valuable lesson in the midst of his decision. Once I give my opinion, I begin to pray that God will have His perfect way.

One of the best books that I ever read on this topic was *Liberated Through Submission* by Bunny Wilson. In this book, I learned that there is freedom in submitting. When William and I don't agree, I express my view, he expresses his view, and I understand that the final decision is up to him. I think it is important for a woman to express her view. Oftentimes, God will put something on a wife's heart that her husband may not have considered. Adding your viewpoint can bring light to a situation or give insight that your husband would have never considered. However, if you hold back your view, he could be missing something very important. A wise man will learn to listen to the viewpoints of his wife. There are things that a wife will discern that will help her husband in decision making. Submission is necessary on both parts.

CHAPTER TWENTY
THE *T* PRINCIPLES

TIME

There are two basic categories of time that I think every married person needs: time together and time alone. Time together can be just the two of you or the two of you and family. It is so important that a husband and wife have regular time together. Time together can be beneficial because this is how you learn more about each other, and it helps you to draw closer. One of God's purposes for marriage is companionship, so spending time together helps to fulfill this purpose.

Don't allow life, the job, the church, or any other entity to kill your time together. We have to be intentional about spending time together, or it just will not happen. Sometimes, my schedule can get so busy that William and I don't get to spend as much time together as I would like. All it takes is a few days of me coming home late or running errands, and before I know it, we are missing each other. When my schedule is so busy that William feels like he hasn't seen me all week, a change must occur. I notice that when we don't have enough time together, we begin to feel distant. So I look at my calendar and make some changes so that I can be home more. Being home and spending time together is important. Time together is precious, and it should be valued.

The second type of time that is essential is time alone. For me, this is time that I get by myself to go for a ride to the store or to the hairdresser, or to get together with a girlfriend. I don't always have to go out of the house to get this time: a nap, bubble bath, or time in a room to read and relax is just as fulfilling.

I think a husband and wife need to be secure enough to allow their spouse some time alone. I heard one husband say, "She doesn't want me to have any time with my friends; she thinks that she should go everywhere that I go." This husband wishes that his wife would give him some time alone and not worry. Time alone helps me to think and become a better me. When I am better, I can be of better help to my husband, children, and anyone else. So time together and time alone are a significant part of a healthy marriage.

TITHE

Will a man or a woman rob God? Most of us would be quick to say no. However, when we are blessed with a job and a source of income and do not give God a tithe and offering from each paycheck, we are robbing God (Malachi 3:8–11). The tithing principle does not make sense to the natural man but the principle works.

When we honor God by giving to Him first and faithfully, He promises to bless our households. God said that He would rebuke the devourer for our sakes. This means that when we give, there is a special protection that He places on our household. There are certain things that He is not going to allow to happen because we have honored Him in our giving. He also says that He will not destroy the fruits of our ground; neither shall our vines drop its fruit before the time (Malachi 3:11). God will allow the things that belong to us to be blessed, items that should break down will often last longer just because God is keeping them working. If He allows something to break down, He will miraculously make a way for the item to be replaced.

I can remember when I was a stay-at-home mom, our refrigerator broke down. I thought, *Lord, we need our refrigerator to work, we don't have the money to buy a new one, so can you please fix this one or miraculously give us another one?* I asked my two children to come and pray with me in front of the broken refrigerator. I asked them, "Do you believe that God is able to fix this refrigerator or give us another one?" They both said yes. The next day, I was talking to my mom and mentioned to her that our refrigerator was not working, and she told me that she was in the process of redecorating her kitchen. She wanted to get rid of all of her appliances and get new ones. She had a refrigerator in perfect condition that she needed to have removed from her kitchen. She asked me if my husband could come and remove it from her house.

Look at God! I had no idea that my mom was redecorating her kitchen and wanted to get rid of her refrigerator. God places a special protection over the homes that honor Him in their giving. In Malachi 3:10, the Lord ask us to bring all the tithe (the whole tenth of your income) "'into the storehouse, that there may be food in My house, and prove Me now by it,' says the Lord of hosts, 'if I will not open the windows of heaven for you and pour you out a blessing, that there shall not be room enough to receive it.'"

Some marriages are facing difficult times just because the household does not honor God by giving tithes and offerings to God's house. Malachi 3:9 says that when we withhold our tithe and offering from God's house, we rob Him. The consequences of robbing God is to be cursed with the curse.

Think about it! God is the one who gives us the ability to get wealth. If it wasn't for Him, we wouldn't have a job or a source of income. It is because of the brain that God put in your head that you are even able to think. He is the one who made your body, every part of it, and if it wasn't for your body, you wouldn't be able to show up for work. So God has given us everything that we have and made it possible for us to collect a paycheck, and then we have the audacity not to honor Him with at least 10 percent of every paycheck. God says that we are robbing Him. This means that we are taking something that doesn't belong to us. He gives us permission to live off of the 90 percent and only asks that we give at least 10 percent of our earnings. When we ignore this principle, we are asking for trouble in our households.

Earlier in Malachi 2:1, He says, "'If you will not hear and if you will not lay it to heart to give glory to My name,' says the Lord of hosts, 'then I will send the curse upon you, and I will curse your blessings; yes, I have already turned them to curses because you do not lay it to heart.'" This verse tells me that when we do not hear and take to heart what this principle is asking us to do, we will be cursed. *Webster's Dictionary* defines *curse* as the expression of a wish that misfortune, evil, and so on befall another. Also, the word *curse* means to be damned, ruined, or bad. Could not honoring this principle have an effect on you and your marriage?

If you have not been one to honor God by obeying this principle, I challenge you to ask God to forgive you. Start honoring God with your very next paycheck or source of income. Before you pay any bill or spend any money, set to the side a tithe and an offering. As you are faithful to God in your giving, you will begin to see the blessings of God like never before. We can't beat God in giving, so as we give to His house, He will give to our house. We can release the curse from our homes by honoring God with our giving. Try God!

TRUST

Blessed is the husband and wife who put their trust in the Lord (Psalm 40:4). When we trust God, we believe Him for every situation in our marriage. We rely on His word to be manifested in our marriage. We believe God to get us from point A to point B. When we trust God, our strength is in Him. We may not be sure of any other area in our marriage but we can be sure that the Lord will take care of us. He will bless us in our marriage as we trust in Him.

Trusting in the Lord has caused me to worry less. Trusting and worrying do not go together. I trust that God knows the plans and the thoughts that He has for my marriage and that He will bring to pass whatever needs to happen.

As I prepared to write this section, I asked the Lord, "What would you like me to share about trust?" I thought a wife should be able to trust her husband and a husband should be able to trust his wife. However, as I sought the Lord and His word, I noticed that I couldn't find one scripture that says a wife must trust her husband or that a husband must trust his wife. Every verse that I came across emphasized the need for us to trust in the Lord. Therefore, I have learned that the only one we can truly have our confidence in is the Lord.

Our husband or our wife may let us down, but the Lord says that He will never leave us nor forsake us. God is reliable, and we can trust Him for every area of our marriage. Rely on Him, depend on Him, and include Him in your marriage. Blessed is the husband and wife who put their trust in the Lord!

TOUCH

One of my husband's requests is that I touch him on a regular basis. The reason that he has to request it is that touching doesn't come naturally to me. I am not a naturally touchy, feely person. I love when my husband holds my hand, rubs my feet, and rubs my back. I receive his touches with no problem, but giving the touches is where I lack. So one of the questions that I ask myself on a regular basis is, "Have I touched my husband today?" He enjoys when I touch him.

I have found that touching is another way to build intimacy. When we go for days without touching, it seems to create distance between us. I know that I haven't been on my job when my husband has to say, "I need you to touch me more." It bothers me when I hear him say this, but I appreciate him letting me know. It reminds me that I have to work on this. When you find that your mate has a need that you can meet, you should do everything within your power to meet the need. However, meeting the need may not be something that comes naturally; therefore, you have to work at it.

Touching can be a great way to build closeness and intimacy, and to stimulate warmth with your mate. I think that everyone is different and may enjoy being touched in different places. Therefore, it is important to communicate about where and how you would like to be touched. If the touch is someplace that you don't enjoy, the touch can be more irritating than anything.

Touching is therapeutic to the body. There is nothing like having a foot rub after being on your feet all day. As husband and wife, we are responsible for providing therapy to each other's body. So I encourage you to make touching a regular part of your marriage.

CHAPTER TWENTY-ONE
THE *U* PRINCIPLES

UNDERSTANDING

I love when I feel that William understands me! The understanding principle is about having knowledge of your mate, being familiar with each other, and realizing that you must use certain skills in dealing with each other, skills like love, affection, care, and so on. Also, use discernment based on what you know about your mate. When a husband and wife have an understanding of each other, the marriage can flow in harmony. Arguments and disagreements will be reduced when you have an understanding of each other. There are certain things that you will not have to fuss or discuss because you have understanding.

Women are so special in the eyes of God. He knew that when He created a woman, she would require special attention. Therefore, in 1 Peter 3:1, God's word instructs husbands to dwell with understanding with their wife. As I read this scripture, I noticed the word *dwell*. The word *dwell* means that a husband is to stay there. God intends for him to always have understanding when dealing with his wife. A husband should be intimately aware of his wife's needs, her strengths, and her weaknesses. He should know her goals and desires. The more that he knows about his wife, the better he will be able to respond to her. Although this works both ways, it is interesting that the scripture focuses on the husband dwelling with understanding.

I believe that understanding comes from God. He made each and every one of us, so why not go to the creator to get an understanding of the creation? God will reveal and help us to understand each other. Proverbs 9:10 says, "The fear of the Lord is the beginning of wisdom, and knowledge of the Holy One is understanding."

UNGODLY

When God made the institution of marriage, I know that it was His desire that a husband and wife be obedient to Him and bring Him glory. Well, Adam and Eve decided to be disobedient, and because of their sin, we all have been affected. Sin creates a problem with us and God, and within ourselves. It can also create a problem for those who love us.

The ungodly principle is all about leaving out the things that do not please God or bring glory and honor to Him. Behaviors that are sinful, wicked, and not acceptable to God should not be practiced. Protect your marriage from ungodly things, people, and places. Where you spend your time and what you do in your leisure time should be a reflection of your relationship with Christ. When you know Christ, your desire should be to please Him.

UNITY

"Behold how good and how pleasant it is for brethren to dwell together in unity" (Psalms 133:1). God said that the two shall be one. One mind, one direction, and one goal creates unity. However, there will be times when you don't feel the unity because you may not be seeing eye to eye on something. When a husband and wife can't see eye to eye on anything, there is no unity. This is why it is so important to date before you get married. Dating should consist of collecting data. The more data you collect, the more you will be able to know about how your partner is thinking, how he or she was raised, and what his or her goals and outlook on life are. Marrying someone who is headed in a totally different direction or who has a totally different mind-set makes unity a difficult task. If a husband and wife are on one accord, there is unity.

When there is unity, there is peace. I believe that communication is the key to unity. The more that you talk to each other, the more you will begin to hear each other's heart, goals, and thoughts. Sharing gives insight and helps you to understand each other. Understanding each other creates harmony and unity. It is a good and pleasant feeling to be in unity with your mate.

UPLIFT

There have been times when I have come home feeling down about something that happened in the course of a day. However, after I have shared it with William, I feel better. It's something about sharing with your husband. He knows me and knows what gets to me; therefore, he knows how to say the right things to uplift me. Now most of the time,

William is pretty good about reading me and knowing when I could use an uplift. When you have been torn down in the world, you should be able to count on being uplifted at home. Loving each other, serving each other, speaking positive words, and praying should be something that we can count on from our mate.

However, Jesus knows and is the only one who will always be available to uplift me when I am down: "I have learned to cast my cares on the Lord because He cares for me" (1 Peter 5:7). When I need to be uplifted, I talk to the Lord and read His word to look for an answer. He gives me an answer, uplifts my spirit, or sends someone to help me.

CHAPTER TWENTY-TWO
THE *V* PRINCIPLES

VACATION

When was the last time that you and your mate went on a vacation? Every marriage needs to experience a time when the husband and wife get away from their daily routine, work, and surroundings to get some rest, relaxation, and fun, and to just enjoy time together. It doesn't have to be an expensive vacation; however, you must plan to do this on a regular basis. There are so many things that we experience in this life that can put a wear and tear on a marriage relationship. Time alone and away from the regular routines can help to refresh and rekindle the romance. Oftentimes, this kind of getaway is not going to come easy. You must be intentional about the planning and the preparation to take a trip. Taking a trip and having time alone can often be the best therapy. So often, we are doing so much with raising a family, working, ministry activities, and everything that time flies and we haven't taken the time to reflect on each other.

Over the past few years, we have planned one vacation with the children and one without the children. I have found that we need time away as a family to relax and have fun. Our children love having this time with us without any other commitments. We relax, swim, play games, tour different places, and just enjoy our family. William and I make it our business to get away together on a retreat or just a weekend getaway. We don't do this as often as we would like because finding childcare is a challenge. However, we make it happen at least once a year. It has made such a difference in our marriage. Life is too short not to take time out and enjoy the mate God has blessed you with.

So I encourage you to get away on a regular basis. Your marriage and your family will be better because of it.

VALIDATE

One of the many things that I was taught by our premarital counselor is that a wife should validate her husband when he is speaking in public.

Your expression will help others to believe your husband and have confidence in what he is saying or doing. I have found this to be true.

You validate him by looking at him when he is speaking and looking in such a way that says, "Yes, he is telling the truth." Oftentimes, when a husband and wife are together and the husband starts to speak, the audience immediately looks at the wife. Although it may not be done verbally, everyone is asking the wife, "Is he telling the truth?" Your expression and your eye contact will either validate what he is saying or it will tell the audience that what he is saying may not be the truth.

Although I was taught this as a wife validating her husband, I have found that it works both ways. When a husband and wife are in public, if the wife speaks, the audience will also look at the husband's face to see if she is telling the truth. So the lesson in this is to watch your expressions when your mate is speaking in public. You will be the key to validating what your mate is saying. The expression that you have while your mate is speaking can make or break the delivery of whatever is being said. Validate your mate.

VARIETY

I didn't always understand what the old saying, "Variety is the spice of life," meant. However, now I understand and have found this statement to be true. Not only true in life but specifically true in married life. Life is exciting when you try different types of experiences. Marriage is exciting when you try different experiences. Variety is compared with spice because a cook uses different spices to create a tasty meal. When the spice is sprinkled in the ingredients, it brings flavor and helps to make a great meal. When a husband and wife are willing to sprinkle some spice into their relationship, it helps to make a great marriage.

There are so many marriages that have been hurt because either the husband or the wife chose to have an affair. When the research is done on why the affair took place, it is often because a husband or a wife wanted some "spice." They were tired of the routine and having the same "meals" the exact same way. They wanted to try something different. They wanted to have a different experience with excitement! There is nothing wrong with wanting to try something different. However, when trying something different means going outside of your marriage and breaking your vows, there is a problem.

After eleven years of marriage, I am finding that variety adds spice to our marriage. One of my friends has done a significant study on the brain. She explained to me that one of the reasons that people have an affair is because there is an area of their brain that is stimulated by the newness of the relationship. When I heard this, I asked, "How can a person who wants to be faithful to their husband or wife get the same kind of stimulation to their brain without having an affair?" She answered by saying that you must be willing to try different things. When a couple who has been married for a while wants to stimulate the area of the brain that craves for something new, they must be willing to add variety to their marriage.

So I started to evaluate my routines and asked myself, "What can I do differently? How can I add some spice to my marriage?" The following are some of the things that I have done to add spice to my marriage:

1. In the kitchen: Cook a different meal, make something different to drink. Add a candle to the table from time to time. Set the table differently.

2. In bed: Wear something that you normally wouldn't wear to bed—something that you know pleases your mate. This may mean not wearing anything at all. Try making love in a different position. If you are not normally the one to initiate, try initiating. Play some romantic music and then make love. Make sure that the atmosphere of your bedroom is set for love.

3. Travel: Be willing to take a trip. Go somewhere that you have never been before. This could be far away or close by. It could be a trip that costs money or one that doesn't cost anything. It could mean going for a walk together.

4. Time together: If you haven't been dating each other, Incorporate a regular date night. Try going to a different place each time. Try a different restaurant. Pray together. God will do a new thing in your relationship.

William and I have recently been spending more time dating each other and trying different things. It has been wonderful! Our marriage has become more interesting and exciting since we have added more variety. Variety really is the spice to life!

VOWS

Do you remember the vows that you made? I can remember saying something like, "I, Carolyn Ausby, take thee, William Tatem, to be my husband, to have and to hold, in sickness and in health, for better or for worse, for richer or for poorer as long as we both shall live." As I observe and speak to couples who have been married for any length of time, they all have experiences to share for each part of the vows.

I have a very close friend who got married as a teenager and has been married for thirty years. She recently experienced a season of sickness and a season of health. Her husband was diagnosed with cancer, and their entire world changed. Her season consisted of going back and forth to the hospital with her husband, making sure that he had the treatment that he needed. She was right by his side all of the way. As he experienced pain in the midnight hour, she was there to comfort him and to pray with him. When he needed to take his medicine, she was there. Who would have ever thought that their marriage would experience a season of sickness? She shared that she has experienced each part of the vows. She went through a season of better or worse, richer or poorer, sickness and health, and then she experienced the death of her husband. With God's help and grace, we can make it through each part of our vows. What God has done for others, He can do for you.

Today, so many couples give up as soon as they experience a part of the vow that doesn't feel good. When money gets low, they split; when the worst happens, they say, "I can't take this." Remember your vows and honor the commitment that you made to God and before all of the people who heard you say your vows (Deuteronomy 23:21).

CHAPTER TWENTY-THREE
THE *W* PRINCIPLES

WAIT

The wedding and the honeymoon is over, now it's time to come home and learn to live together. As you deal with each other on a daily basis, I guarantee you will see your mate do something that you do not like or that you think should be done differently. It could be something simple like dropping dirty clothes on the floor instead of placing them in the dirty clothes hamper. It could be leaving the toilet seat up when you feel that it should be down. Perhaps you would like to receive a phone call during the day to know that your mate is all right, but your mate is not used to checking in. Let's say that your mate has a habit of using the automatic teller machine without letting you know that money is gone. So you can never really know what is in your bank account. This begins to create other problems. Whatever the case may be, there will be some differences.

The differences require us to WAIT. Living the married life will require us to wait. We will not always get what we want when we want it. The wait principle is all about learning to wait on God to create a change in us, in our mate, or in our situation.

When we begin to see and experience the differences, we have to decide whether or not we are going to talk about them or let them go. I have found that it is good to communicate your desires, but don't expect change right away. Your mate can either receive what you are saying or reject what you are saying. Sometimes, he will receive what you are saying, but he may have done something for so long that it is hard to break the habit. We must realize that there are so many things that we learn to do before we are married. We come into our marriage doing those things that we have always done and that may be the very thing that irritated our mate. So when we learn that they are irritated, we may decide that we will do things differently. Sometimes, a change will come, and sometimes, it will not. However, you have to learn to wait without having a bad attitude. I have seen God change my husband in certain areas over time. There are a lot of things that he didn't do when we first got married; however, he does them now. When I see God change William in a certain area, I give God praise because He is faithful. We must be patient with each other because God is patient with us. I am sure that there are a lot of things that God wants us to do, but He is waiting on us to get it. While He is waiting, He is still good to us and He keeps on blessing us. While we are waiting on our mate to change in a certain area, we have to learn to still be good and continue to bless each other.

Resist the temptation to nag. Nagging will only make it worse. Once you have discussed your desire for something to be done differently, prayer is the next step. Talking to God about the desire is the most effective action to take. God is the only person who can create a positive change in our mate. He will cause us to do things that we never thought were possible. So don't get frustrated, impatient, and upset; pray about it and WAIT! God is able to create a change. If God doesn't change your mate, He will often change you or your attitude toward the situation.

WEDDING RING

Imagine how lost we would be if there weren't any signs. A stop sign tells us when to stop. Oftentimes, when we are driving, we don't actually read the sign because we automatically know that when we see the red and white sign, it means stop. Usually, when we stop, we look and then we proceed. Well, your wedding ring should be worn every day on your finger as a sign.

Do you wear your wedding ring? The ring is a visual sign for you and anyone who sees you. The sign should be seen and interpreted as "This person is married, taken, and not interested in allowing anyone to fill my mate's shoes." When we get married, we become one. Wherever we go, we no longer represent just ourselves; if we are a wife, we represent our husband, and if we are a husband, we represent our wife. Most importantly, the both of you should be representing Christ. He created marriage, and your marriage should be a reflection of Him. You may have to physically go somewhere without your spouse. This is why you should always wear your ring. Your ring is a visual sign to the world that "I am one with someone." Your ring says, "I am taken." You need to know this, and your actions should say the same.

Just like with street signs, some people don't read them. Sometimes, people of the opposite sex will not see your ring or will not read the ring sign. They will ignore it and try to see if your actions indicate that you are taken. It is up to you to present yourself in such a way that your ring and your actions are saying the same thing: "I am taken." You shouldn't want to be seen without it.

The wedding ring is a precious sign that symbolizes a transfer of authority, strength, and protection. It is a circle that represents the everlasting love of God and the love that He wants us to have in our marriage. It is a constant reminder to you that you made a commitment to your spouse until death. Let the world know that you belong to someone; you are taken, not available. Wear your ring!

WITHHOLD

"Do not withhold good from those to whom it is due, when it is in the power of your hand to do so" (Proverbs 3:27). In a marriage between a husband and wife, there are certain things that we owe to each other, Such as love, affection, attention, and so on. So why do we withhold these things, knowing that they are due and that we have the power to give them?

Sometimes, there are issues in marriage that cause us to withhold. You feel like since you are not getting this, then you are not giving that. I can remember a time that we were going through an issue that lasted for a few years. I felt like my husband was not hearing me, he was handling the issue his way, and I just had to deal with it. Well, one of the ways that it unconsciously affected me was that it created tightness in our intimacy. I was not free in bed because I felt like a part of me was not being heard. I don't believe in denying my husband; however, I was not free in the bed because deep down, I felt that I was being ignored on an issue that was very important. After a few years, this issue was addressed and resolved. My husband finally did what I had requested of him to handle the issue, and he said that he noticed the difference in the bedroom. I wasn't intentionally holding back, but deep down it bothered me that my husband was not hearing me, and it affected me in the bedroom. There is a freedom that comes upon you when you feel heard, understood and honored.

So what am I saying? Do not withhold from your mate when it is within your power to do so. Think of something that you know your spouse wants from you; it could be something as simple as going for a walk in the park. When it is in your power to do it, why not do it? Life is too short. Tomorrow is not promised; don't hold back on giving your mate all that is due.

WORDS

What kind of words have you been speaking to your husband or wife? Are they words that build up, encourage, or strengthen, or words that are tearing down? What you say from day to day means a lot. If we all learn to bridle our tongue in our marriages, many of the arguments or disagreements that we have would be reduced by a great percentage. To *bridle* means to restrain, to limit, or to control. The Bible says that if anyone among you thinks he is religious, and does not bridle his tongue but deceives his own heart, this one's religion is useless (James 1:26). God wants us to watch our mouths. He gives us power to bridle our tongue; we must use it. Once you say the words out of your mouth, you can't take them back. Don't say everything you think, but please think about everything that you say. Ask yourself, will the words that I am about say help to build or tear down? As children, we used to say, "Sticks and stones may break my bones but words will never hurt me." This statement is so far from the truth because words do hurt. Oftentimes, the words will be played over and over in your head long after the disagreement is over. The devil will keep reminding you of the negative words that were said.

We have experienced various situations in our marriage that have been challenging. There have been times where we have made decisions and the plans did not work out as we thought. When a problem arises, we could easily blame each other and exchange words that would not be pleasant. Have you ever wanted to just tell your mate off? We have found that when we learn to bridle our tongue, God is able to speak on our behalf. He may send someone else to share the same word with your mate, or He may speak directly to your mate. We must be selective in the words that we speak. How, when, and what you say is crucial! Know that you will give account for every word that comes out of our mouth (Matthew 12:36).

Learn to take the compliments to your mate and the criticism to God. God is the only one who can fix the areas that need to be changed. As you pray about the changes that you would like to see in your mate,

God will either change your mate or change you. I have prayed about certain characteristics that I would like to see in my mate, and have seen God make him over. We must be patient because oftentimes, the change does not occur over night.

WORRY

Have you ever spent time worrying about your future, your finances, your spouse, your children, or anything? During the course of a marriage, there will be some unexpected things or situations that take place. I can guarantee you that something will happen to shift the level of comfort that you once had in your marriage.

Perhaps someone loses a job, someone gets sick, a decision is made that negatively affects your family, death takes place, or something happens to one of your children. When these situations occur, the human mind begins to worry. Questions like, "How will we get out of this situation?" "How will our needs be met?"

I can remember when we first made the decision for me to leave my job and come home to raise our two children. I had been working my entire life, and the thought of leaving my job and coming home to live on one income was not appealing to me. However, I was sure that God was calling me home to raise my children, and my husband was in agreement. This decision moved me from a level of comfort to one of worrying. I began to worry about how we were going to make it; will my kids have everything they need? However, God taught me how to move from worrying to trust and faith in Him. I learned to trust God like never before. I prayed about many things that I used to take for granted, like the bills and the mortgage being paid. God never ceased to amaze me. He blessed exceedingly and abundantly above all that I could have ever asked or thought. He took care of us in such an amazing way the entire time that I was home with my children.

To worry is to feel uneasy, to fret, or to be anxious about something. It can also mean tormenting oneself or suffering from disturbing thoughts. In Matthew 6:25–34, Jesus teaches about worry. He tells us not to worry about our life, what we will eat or drink, or about our body and what we will wear. The alternative that He gives for worrying is to seek first His kingdom and His righteousness and all these things will be given to you (Matthew 6:33). When unexpected situations hit your marriage, you can count on God to be right there. He already knows what has caused the worry, but He has instructed us not to worry. We must immediately turn our minds and hearts toward God. God wants to have first place in your mind and your thoughts. Trust God to take care of every situation in your marriage.

CHAPTER TWENTY-FOUR
THE *X, Y,* AND *Z* PRINCIPLES

X-RAY

One of the things that I have found to be true in every marriage that I have encountered is that every husband and wife brings something into their marriage based on what was observed or experienced in their childhood. This could be good or bad. For example: My husband grew up having meals at the table. He enjoyed all of his family coming together at mealtime. Therefore, when we first got married, he made it clear to me that he wanted us to have all of our meals at the table. I didn't have any problem with this. However, I didn't grow up having every meal at the table. Sometimes, we would have our dinner on a tray and eat while watching something on TV. Everyone would gather at the table for special holidays like Thanksgiving or Christmas.

Another example (true story, but different names): Shawn and Sheila get married in a hurry. They fall in love and don't spend much time in counseling; they decide to get married after dating for a few weeks. Sheila hopes that this is Mr. Right and plans to be married forever. However, Shawn was raised in a home where he saw his mom get married several times. The message that Shawn has is that if something goes wrong, or doesn't work out, just get a divorce. Shawn has brought this same mentality into his marriage because this is what he experienced as a child. He may not even know why he jumps in and out of relationships. Some people have never taken the time to stop and evaluate why they do some of the things that they do.

This is why an x-ray is necessary. To x-ray is to take time to examine, investigate, inspect, or carefully inquire about why you do the things that you do. As I have listened to numerous couples share problems that they face in their marriage, I have noticed that so many of the problems connect to things that they saw, heard, or experienced in their childhood. We really should x-ray ourselves before we get into marriage so that we can work on things or attitudes that may not be healthy in a marriage. It is unfortunate that some things don't show up on the x-ray until after we are married. When this happens, you may not like what you see or the person you have married. However, this is when our vows "for better or for worse" come in. Some x-rays show that as a child you were exposed to some great things like family-oriented support, self-esteem, perseverance, godly parents and good role models. Some x-rays show some negative things like verbal abuse, physical abuse, drug abuse, alcoholism, rape and divorce. If these issues are not dealt with, they will create a problem in your marriage.

The problems do not get erased when you become an adult; they are still there. There are so many children with issues who grow into adults who are walking around with the same issues. They may have never told anyone about them, but they are carrying them. It is not until they are x-rayed that the issue comes out. God will reveal some of these things as you are dating, and it is up to you to take notice. Sometimes, He reveals the issues but we ignore them. We hope that it will be better after we are married; however, the issue is often magnified after we get married. The good news is that God is able to heal and restore anything that the x-ray reveals. Hang in there!

THE "Y" PRINCIPLE

YOU

James and Janet have been married for twenty-five years. They look good on the outside. They are an attractive couple, they are involved in ministry together, they live in a beautiful home, and both have a relationship with the Lord. However, Janet is not happy because she has experienced some things with James that need to be changed. She wants him to change. She has expressed her concerns over and over again, but nothing has changed. She told me that she has prayed and waited, but he still has not changed. I tried to encourage her with God's word, but she basically said, "I have been there and done that, and he still has not changed." How many of you ladies can relate to this?

Well, God's word is applicable to every situation that we can ever face in our marriage. It is a trick of the devil to make us belittle the word of God and prayer. God's word will not return void. His word is truth. When you are waiting on God to change your mate and you don't see any change, that is often a sign that God wants to change you. You can't make a change occur in your spouse. Only God has the power to make a person change. Perhaps He wants to change you in the midst of the situation or change your reaction, the way that you handle the situation. In 1 Peter 3:1 it says that a man can be changed by the conduct of his wife. You and your conduct have everything to do with the changes that will occur in your marriage. Jesus also said, "Therefore with loving kindness I have drawn you" (Jeremiah 31:3). What are you doing to orchestrate a change? Many of us try to use our mouths by nagging, or having a bad attitude toward our mates when we want them to change. Some even shut down intimately because until the change takes place, they can't fully embrace their mate. Imagine if God were to treat us this way. He didn't wait until we changed to die on the cross. He died while we were still in sin. He paid the price before we got here.

So when you see a change that needs to occur in your marriage or in your mate, let the change start with you. Seek God, read God's word, and pray. Romans 12:2 says, "Be transformed by the renewing of your mind." This is where the change begins. Start renewing your mind, and your conduct will follow. When you begin to let God change you, you will see results. He will change your situation and your mate when you change. So if you have been praying for a change in your mate, and the change has not occurred, let God change you!

THE "Z" PRINCIPLE

ZEBRA

The last principle is the *Z* principle. The *Z* stands for Zebra. As I spent a little time researching the zebra, I learned that zebras and marriages have a few things in common. Zebras are known as African equids; they have distinctive white and black stripes. Their stripes come in different patterns unique to each individual. Every marriage has its own black and white stripes. The black stripes represent its dark days. Dark days are days when you may not get along, communication could be off, someone may have lost a job or a family member, or someone may just be going through a trial. The white stripes represent the bright days. The bright days are when everything is going great, you are treating each other wonderfully, the intimacy level is high, you had a wonderful date or vacation together, and so on. Anyone who has been married for any length of time knows that there will be some black stripes and some white stripes. Each marriage has its own unique pattern, and no marriage is exactly the same.

When I dreamed of marriage, I only dreamed about the white stripes. I don't think that I ever thought that there would be black stripes. However, the two stripes must go together to make up the zebra's distinctive coat. In the marriage institution, God had to give us both colored stripes. The white stripes are wonderful, but it's the dark stripes that teach us how to lean and depend on God in our marriage. The dark stripes help us to get closer to God and to learn more about Him. If all we ever had were white stripes, we probably would feel like we could handle the marriage all by ourselves. Marriage is God's institution, and just like zebras, each one is unique. God wants to be included in our marriages, so thank Him for the black and the white stripes! It is the stripes that cause us to look to Him. So regardless of the stripes that you face, hang in there, don't give up. The black and the white stripes make the zebra a beautiful animal!

CLOSING

I love marriage and I see it as a wonderful institution created by God. I realize that in order for me to function well in my marriage, I must include God. God sent His word as an instruction book for how to maintain a healthy and happy marriage. In today's society, we often hear so much about getting married and planning a wedding, but not enough about how to maintain a healthy and happy marriage on a day to day basis. When I got married, I only thought about the good days and how great it would be. Through premarital counseling and studying God's word pertaining to marriage, I was given tools and principles to help through the day to day challenges of a marriage. Sometimes it's just the little things that can be done to make a big difference. I pray that the principles in this book will bless you. I challenge you to apply the principles from A to Z. God's word works.

CPSIA information can be obtained
at www.ICGtesting.com
Printed in the USA
LVOW10s1009220117
521763LV00002B/334/P